Making Soup

DIY Bath & Body Products Made with All-Natural Scents, Oils, and Colors

AGNES STUBER

TRANSLATED BY GUN PENHOAT

Skyhorse Publishing

Foreword

Soapmaking is equal parts chemistry and artistry. The nerdy natural scientist side of me cheers, and my inner artist does as well.

Never before have we been so aware of the importance of clean hands. Soap hasn't really received the same recognition as that given to hand sanitizers; even though soap is just as good, and in some cases, even better than other disinfectants. Alcohol-based hand sanitizers, for example, won't protect against calicivirus (a norovirus). This virus is often referred to as "the winter vomiting bug" because the outbreaks are seasonal and most common during winter months. It's important to wash our hands thoroughly with soap and water because the norovirus is enclosed in a fatty membrane, which soap dissolves. Not many inventions have saved as many lives as wonderfully as soap.

This book consists of several chapters, some of which contain chemistry jargon. Perhaps this gives the impression that making soap is a complex and difficult science, requiring hard studying to learn. But no, it's really very simple to make soap. You must, of course, have safety measures in place. Once that's done, just mix lye and oil, and there you have it, soap! If you wish, dig deep into the science to learn all about fatty acids, additives, and fragrances. However, you can make it incredibly easy on yourself by just collecting the necessary tools: sodium hydroxide, oils, and containers to pour the soap into.

Soapmaking is such a great hobby because you can create endless variations of soaps by changing patterns and scents. We all need to wash our hands, so it is also a useful hobby, different from collecting stamps or watches, for comparison. (Both my brothers are such collectors and it is totally okay with me, but admittedly, I don't see the charm.) I truly believe that soapmaking is a hobby where you mix usefulness with pure pleasure.

Agnes

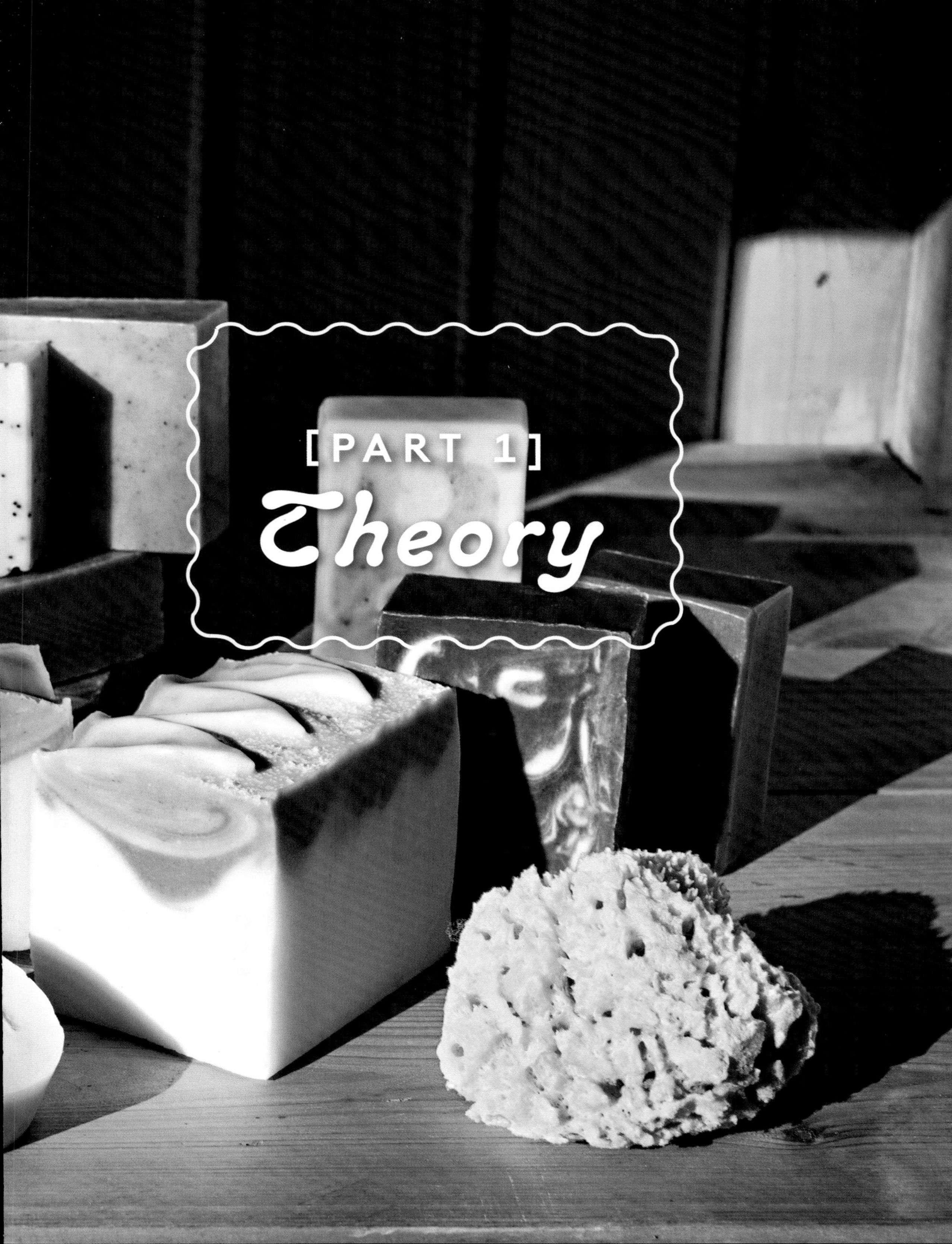

[PART 1] Theory

Soapmaking terminology

CP, COLD PROCESS. Soap is made by mixing room-temperature oils with lye.

CPOP, COLD PROCESS/OVEN PROCESS. Cold process soap is placed in the oven to force it to gel.

DOS, DREADED ORANGE SPOTS. Small orange spots caused by rancid oils or unsaponified oils that have had prolonged exposure to oxidative stress.

EO, ESSENTIAL OILS. Highly concentrated aromatic liquids extracted from different plant materials and used as fragrance.

FO, FRAGRANCE OIL. Fragrances can contain both essential oils and artificial oils.

GELLING, GEL PHASE. Soap mixture that is very hot enters a gelling phase, i.e. the soap is gelling. Colors become brighter and the soap's shelf life is increased.

HP, HOT PROCESS. Soap ingredients are mixed while heated, often in a slow cooker.

INSULATION. This is to keep the soap batter uniformly warm. Can be done by wrapping the mold in a blanket or setting the mixture on a heating plate or in the oven.

KOH. Potassium hydroxide mixed with water makes lye and produces liquid soap.

MP/M&P, MELT AND POUR. Commercial ready-made soap base that is melted to make soap with your own choice of additives.

PPO, PER POUND OF OILS. Extremely common expression in soapmaking for how to calculate ratios of different additives. 1 pound = 453.5 grams. I have rounded this up to 500 grams for calculations in this book.

SF, SUPERFAT. Superfat is the percentage of free-floating oils that are not turned into soap but stay in their original state. The resulting soap is milder and less dehydrating.

SODA ASH/SODIUM CARBONATE. It is very common that the lye reacts to oxygen and produces a thin ash-like layer on the soap. This is not dangerous but doesn't look very nice.

TRACE, TRACING. When you mix an alkaline compound (lye for example) with oils, the mixture starts to emulsify—saponification starts. The soap mixture thickens in stages and traces can be seen on the surface.

SURFACTANTS. Chemical products that act as wetting agents and lower the surface tension. Even "real" soap lowers surface tension so it is really a surfactant.

SAPONIFICATION. The process of making soap.

A Dirty Story

According to one legend, *soap* got its English name after Mount Sapo, where the Ancient Romans conducted animal sacrifice. Animal fat mixed with ash from the fires created a kind of primitive soap that leaked into the River Tiber below, where the washerwomen noticed the clothes came out cleaner. This is just a myth, more's the pity. The Latin word for fat, *sebum*, is the real word origin. It is doubtful that the Romans had a habit of burning edible animal carcasses; and there is no Mount Sapo.

Soap has been around for a very long time, even if it took until the middle of the nineteenth century for humans to realize how important it is for our health. The first description of a soap product is from 2800–2500 BC, before the last woolly mammoth had gone extinct (2500–2000 BC), in the same era the Egyptians created the 365-day calendar and built the Cheops Pyramid. In Mesopotamia, the Sumerians recorded on clay tablets a recipe for a concoction made from ash and fat. The recipe said to mix oils and wood ash and heat the mixture. Wood ash acts as a disinfectant and its use is still recommended by the World Health Organization (WHO) when there is no soap available.

"Soap [Sapo] is also an invention of the Gallic provinces for making the hair red. It is made from suet and ash. The best is from beech ash and goat suet, in both thick and liquid consistencies used among the Germans, more by men than by women."
FROM THE ROMAN PLINY THE ELDER'S *NATURAL HISTORY* WHERE HE EXPLAINS HOW TO USE SOAP AS A WRAP FOR A SORE THROAT.

The earliest use of soap was limited to washing wool fibers, spreading later to medicinal and cosmetic use in certain geographical areas.

Greek physician Galenos wrote around 100 AD [CE] that soap didn't just possess healing properties, but could also remove dirt from the body and clothes. The Romans don't seem to have had any use for soap even though they had an affinity for frequenting communal bathhouses. After the fall of the Roman Empire, people stopped bathing and, as a consequence, everybody lived through many dirty years with serious illnesses like the Black Death.

The next important milestone in the history of soap came when Arabs used burnt lime as an alkaline component, which produced a harder soap. They brought this knowledge with them to the Mediterranean regions where this method spread. Today, the Mediterranean is still well-known for soapmaking.

Mediterranean countries have the advantage of being in proximity to the sea. This provides two very good ingredients for soapmaking: soda ash (more commonly known as sodium carbonate) from burning sea vegetation, and olive oil from olive groves.

> "He hath cast me into the mire, and I am become like dust and ashes."
> JOB 30:19

But why use ash? The decoction is called lye, a strongly alkaline blend, which works as a cleaning solution. Wearing protective rubber gloves, you can use lye to clean clothes, windows, and other surfaces. Lye has long been used for cleaning textiles, although most people today opt for commercial washing powder. However, lye use is becoming popular again with allergy sufferers and because of environmental concerns (for example, in Beneficio, an intentional community in southern Spain, whose members try to live outside of high-tech society).

The progress of potash

If you dry boil ash you'll get potash, also called potassium carbonate. Potash was once a very important ingredient in soapmaking. Lye can be created by pouring boiling water over potash. Leave potash to steep for several days or boil ash in water for a few hours. To return the mixture to potash, just let the water evaporate until only dry ash is left.

In the sixteenth century, Queen Christina of Sweden gave Swedish aristocrat Hugo Hamilton permission to operate a potash distillery and soap-boiling factory. Subsequently, many similar enterprises started up, and they bought their potash from farmers. Potash became an important revenue source for both sharecroppers and farmers. Taxes could even be paid with potash during this period. Female soap-boilers traveled between households offering their services, and soap was mixed and made from slaughter waste.

> "Then a fire is lit, and it burns strongly until the ash glows red hot and starts to run, and you break apart the wooden logs with tall rods, then hit them with paddles to remove the ash while it is still red hot so it becomes packed down hard as a stone or a lump. Once this bluish, dark, and slag-like ash has cooled down it is brought to the towns and sold."
>
> CARL VON LINNÉ

Sweden was the leading exporter of potash during the seventeenth and eighteenth centuries. Unfortunately, it was used primarily for the manufacturing of gunpowder, not to care for bodily hygiene. Potash burning was not, to say the least, a sustainable industry. It contributed to the disappearance of Sweden's beech forests in the nineteenth century.

Nicolas LeBlanc, a Frenchman, patented a revolutionary discovery in 1791 with a means to extract sodium bicarbonate from common table salt (sodium chloride). Ironically, the French Revolution caused him to lose his factory and led him to commit suicide. The Solvay process, invented by Belgian chemist Ernest Solvay, replaced the LeBlanc process in 1861. The Solvay process is still used today in the manufacturing of sodium carbonate.

In the second half of the nineteenth century, the germ theory of disease (the currently accepted scientific theory for many diseases) began to win respect, and people started to wash their hands. Ignaz Semmelweis, a Hungarian physician and early proponent of handwashing, discovered that the maternal mortality rate increased when physicians performed autopsies just before assisting in childbirth. He studied the problem and, after recommending handwashing, there was a drastic reduction in maternal mortality. Unfortunately, not all of his peers agreed, and Ignaz Semmelweis didn't receive deserved recognition until much later. If only he could see how diligently we wash our hands today!

Invention of tenside soap

Soapmaking suffered during WWI and WWII because of a lack of fats and oils. Industrial artificial detergents (more commonly known as tensides) were invented. Tensides are surfactants, and soap belongs to them, even if the name is primarily used today when talking about synthetic soap. Starting in 1954, more tenside detergents were produced than soap detergents. Tenside-based shampoo arrived in the 1960s, and we started using liquid synthetic soap in the 1990s.

Chemically speaking, these are not true soaps. Different additives like fatty alcohols, lecithin, sorbitol, parabens, formaldehyde, and others are needed to create synthetic soap. The glycerin that forms is often separated out, as it is very expensive, and replaced with a small amount of cheaper glycerin. Some people might be sensitive to tenside soaps because of these synthetic ingredients. Artificial soaps are also called SynDet (synthetic detergent) bars. Dove is a SynDet bar, as are Lush soaps, which imitate artisanal soaps.

Artisanal soap

This is soap in a nutshell: fat reacts with an alkaline solution, like sodium hydroxide, and the results are soap and glycerin.

$C_3H_5(O_2CR)_3$	+	$_3MOH$	$\rightarrow$	$_3RC_2OM$	+	$C_3H_5(OH)_3$
fat	+	alkaline solution	$\rightarrow$	soap	+	glycerol
triglycerides	+	hydroxide ions	$\rightarrow$	fatty acid ions (soap ions)	+	glycerol (glycerin)

What we call soap is really sodium salt. (If soap is made with potassium hydroxide, the result is potassium salt, also known as soft soap, a universal household cleaner.) Glycerin, a humectant, is a by-product naturally occurring in fat that is often added to skincare products for its moisturizing effect.

Soap is a surfactant that lowers the surface tension on water. Pin-shaped soap molecules have one hydrophobic end (which repels water) and one hydrophilic end (which attracts water). The hydrophobic end prefers to link up with fats and oils. The hydrophilic end adheres to water, rests on top of the fat droplets, and makes them loosen their hold. Dirt, bacteria, and viruses are then rinsed off with running water.

Artisanal handmade soap is kinder to the skin than industrial soap, as it retains glycerin and is also superfatted (i.e., this soap contains oils that have not been saponified, so they stay in their original state). This makes it possible to create extra mild soaps for hypersensitive skin and different dermatological conditions. However, it is important to keep in mind that, whether industrially produced or handmade, all soap will be dehydrating to a certain extent. This is necessary for it to have cleaning properties.

There are loads of soap recipes to try for different purposes. Additives and color-and-scent mixtures can be combined in multiple ways. We are all different, so what works for me perhaps won't work for someone else. A soap recipe might be too cleansing and dehydrating for one person, or the texture might be too soft or scratchy. Hopefully this book will provide you with a good foundation in soapmaking so you can make your own modifications and arrive at your own favorite recipes.

The Process

Soapmaking methods

COLD PROCESS

Cold process is currently the most common soapmaking method. Cold process means the soap ingredients are not heated but mixed at room temperature. This doesn't mean that the ingredients need to be *at* room temperature *or* cold, because sodium hydroxide mixed with water produces a lot of heat.

Lye and water ought to hold about the same temperature when they are mixed. Keep in mind that any oils and butters still need to be melted. Aim for an ingredient temperature between 73.4°F–114.8°F (23°C– 46°C).

Pour the soap batter into a mold and insulate it with a blanket, or if you don't want the soap to gel, place it in a refrigerator, cold garage, or cupboard. You can also leave the soap batter at room temperature, but there is a slight risk of partial gelling, which will affect the look of the soap. The reason for this is that the center of the soap batter is warmest, so if the batter doesn't receive any exterior heat, and the soap is not kept evenly warm, it can lead to gelling of only the interior, which will remain darker.

OVEN-HEATED COLD PROCESS

This is the next step in the cold process. Once you have poured the soap batter into a mold, place the mold in the oven. This is to force the whole mixture to gel.

Gelling can be done without an oven, but there is more uncertainty when and how it happens. The soap becomes very warm during the gel phase. Allowed to gel, soap becomes more shelf-stable and the colors are more vibrant. You can remove the soap from the mold sooner, but it still needs to cure.

Avoid gelling if using ingredients with natural sugars like beer, milk, or honey. These produce excessive heat which might make the soap crack or "volcano" out of the mold.

Avoid putting the mixture in the oven if you use a high volume (above 50 percent) of coconut oil in your soap. This mixture heats up and gels very fast. Wrapping the mold in a blanket should be enough.

HOT PROCESS

Hot process is another way to make soap. As the name suggests, you add heat while ingredients are mixed in a saucepan or, preferably, a slow cooker. This is probably the method most people associate with soapmaking—picture an enormous vat with a soapmaker stirring a simmering mixture with a long pole.

With hot process, you have more control over which oil is used for superfat because the additives and extra oil are added once the soap mixture is already saponified. Be aware, the texture of hot process soap is not as smooth as the texture of cold process soap. Hot process gives a coarser and more rustic result. Some people believe that hot process soap doesn't need to cure, that it can be used as soon as it is cut up. However, this soap needs to rest, preferably 4–6 weeks, just like cold process soap.

MELT & POUR SOAP MIXTURE

You may have experimented with ready-made soap batter, the so-called melt and pour soap base that is sold in hobby stores. This is not true soap but rather a synthetic mixture that you melt and add different additives to. This is a good first step or simpler alternative if you want to make soap with children. Avoid using lye with melt and pour soap bases.

Saponification

Saponification is an exciting process that starts when oil and lye are mixed together, resulting in an exothermic (heat creating) chemical reaction. The soap batter can reach in excess of 176°F (80°C) during saponification.

Saponification may take a few hours, up to 48 hours, depending on the oils you're using. The most common duration is around 24 hours. This process is complete when then there is no longer any lye present, only soap and glycerin (and some oil because of superfatting). In other words, the soap is safe to use, but it isn't quite ready yet!

Tracing

Tracing happens during saponification. Saponification begins as soon as you mix oil and lye and, as you continue to mix, the batter thickens and leaves visible traces on the surface.

Compare it to the stages when whipping cream: First it is soft, then a bit thicker, and finally it forms stiff peaks. Whisk the cream too much and you'll get butter. Similarly, the soap batter can trace so much that it becomes nearly impossible to press into a mold.

Tracing is divided into light, medium, and heavy trace stages. Emulsion is the first stage before tracing actually starts, when oil and lye are properly mixed but the mixture has not started to thicken. There are no absolute thresholds for when one stage enters the next. It can happen at different speeds. It also depends on how hard you mix.

Light trace stage is recognizable by oily traces that appear when you stir the soap mixture with the immersion blender. Light trace appears a bit like oil on water's surface. It might be difficult to see depending on lighting. If you want a light trace for a specific pattern, and want to make sure that the mixture is starting to trace, just lift up the immersion blender. If the oily sheen doesn't break on the head of the blender, and the mixture is smooth and not grainy, it is emulsified. If you continue to mix you will see a "skin" develop, resembling that on top of warm milk.

Blend some more and the mixture enters the medium trace stage. You'll notice on the immersion blender that the mixture is getting thicker. If you lift up the blender and let drops fall onto the soap surface, the drops won't penetrate the mixture completely.

If you continue mixing, or let the soap stand a while, it will enter the heavy trace stage. You might desire this stage for certain patterns; stirring the soap mixture leaves strong traces that stay.

If you stir the batter too much, or let it stand too long, it will become too hard and difficult to easily pour into the mold. This can also happen with acceleration, i.e., when the batter traces superfast because it contains additives like honey. The soap is still good, but you might need to forcibly press it into the mold, which might create ugly air pockets.

To slow down tracing, mix oils and lye when they are at a lower temperature, all the way down to room temperature. You can also add more water and/or liquid oils to the recipe.

FALSE TRACE

Soap batter can be tricky. If the mixture hardens without hardly any stirring at all, but the oil and lye are still separated, looking more like lumps that have thickened, check the exterior temperature on the mixing bowl: The trace is not real if you don't feel any heat (which should be produced at the start of saponification).

If you pull up the blender and instead of a smooth mixture layer on the blender head, it's grainy, stop using the immersion blender and continue to stir with a spatula until the oil and lye are properly mixed.

False trace can happen if saponification is done at low temperatures with very thick oils like coconut or wax because they have time to begin hardening. The solution is to saponify at room temperature. Adapt the ingredients' temperature to their melting point so that they don't have time to harden too soon.

Honestly, I was very worried about false trace when I first started making soap, but I have not experienced it even once, so don't let it frighten you.

Temperature

Temperature is very important in soapmaking. Heat is created when sodium hydroxide and water are mixed to lye. The lye needs to cool to below 122°F (50°C), preferably lower. There should be no more than 50°F (10°C) difference when oils and lye are being mixed.

Ingredients at room temperature, around 69.8°F–71.6°F (21°C–22°C), can go through saponification, but I feel that temperature is optimal around 78.8°F–104°F (26°C–40°C). The lye is often slightly warmer than the oils, but it doesn't matter as long as there isn't too much of a temperature difference.

Heat is produced again once saponification starts. It can be controlled by either cooling down the soap or heating it. To heat it, wrap it in a blanket or place it in the oven. The soap mixture should not go above 194°F (90°C), which is too warm for saponification. However, it can't get so cold that it freezes, because then it can't go through saponification either. Primarily, soap with high sugar content can get so hot that it needs to be cooled down in the refrigerator, which prevents it from burning or creating a soap volcano.

Curing

Soap is not ready even if the oils and lye are saponified in about 24 hours. Soap needs to cure for at least 4 weeks, preferably a bit longer, depending on the amount of water and which oils are in the recipe.

Soap hardens and water evaporates during curing. The purpose of water in the recipe is to make mixing the sodium hydroxide with the oils possible. Most of the water will evaporate during the following weeks. How much depends on the humidity where you store the soap. The evaporation will cause the soap to weigh a bit less than when you cut it up. Do a test by weighing newly cut soap, then weigh it again a few weeks or months later.

Now, this is not all that happens! During curing, a crystallization process occurs in which the soap molecules rearrange themselves and form nice crystals (unfortunately not visible to the naked eye) that harden the soap. This takes a while because different soap molecules, made from different fatty acids, harden at different paces. Some soap molecules just need a little bit more time to produce nice crystals.

Why do we want hard soap? It improves shelf life and gives better texture and lather. An uncured soap is fine for washing your hands, but it will be soft, not last very long, and will lather poorly.

Something else happens during curing. Sodium hydroxide gives hand-made soap a high pH level but the pH is reduced somewhat during curing, so the longer the soap is cured, the milder it becomes.

Four to six weeks is a good guideline for most soap curing. It is not really possible to pinpoint an exact moment when the soap is sufficiently cured, as it depends on many factors. If you want to nitpick, you can always say that curing is never really completely done. A pure olive soap, for example, needs to cure for a year to arrive at the same shelf life that a soap made from several oils will have attained after a few weeks.

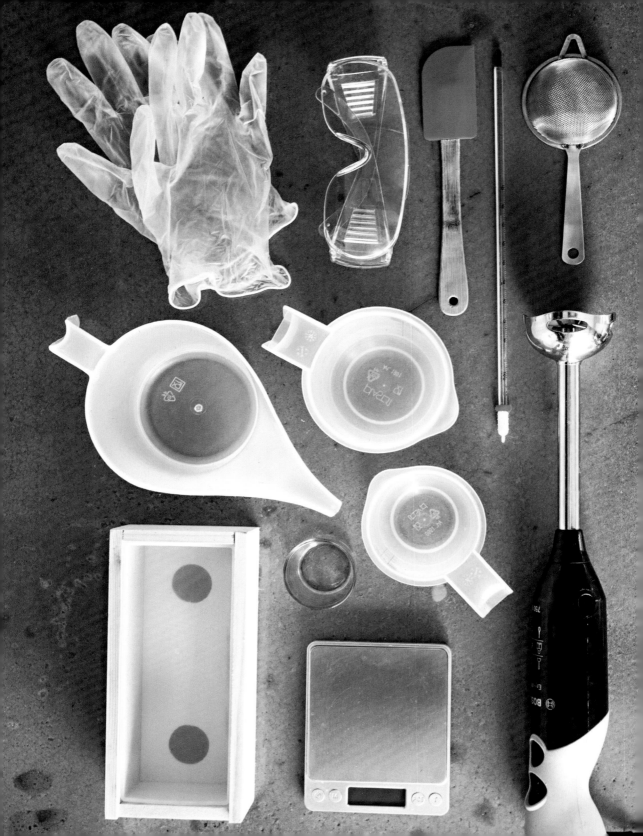

Tools

There are a few necessary tools you'll need for making soap:

MOLD. Something to pour the soap into. Don't use glass, as it might crack, or aluminum, as it reacts with lye. Most other materials are fine. You can line your mold with parchment paper.

SAFETY EQUIPMENT. Safety glasses and protective gloves in rubber or plastic; washing-up gloves work fine.

SPATULA. A super tool specifically for saponification.

IMMERSION BLENDER. It is possible to mix soap by hand, but it will take so much longer. An immersion blender is your best friend for saving time and to stop you from getting a sore arm.

THERMOMETER. Preferably an infrared thermometer, so you don't have to immerse it in lye and oils, but any thermometer will do.

JUG. Either in food contact–compliant plastic or stainless steel.

SCALES. Kitchen scales are fine but preferably one that shows single grams to get the most precise weight possible. My scales have a capacity of 3,000 grams (6.61 pounds), which works for both small and large soap batches.

Not all of the following tools are must-haves, but they make things so much easier:

SIEVE. Lye often needs to be strained when it is poured into oils. Invisible remnants of old soap or other things can stick to the jug and lie like a stiff layer or create small flakes in the lye. A sieve helps strain out these remnants.

RAG. A designated piece of cloth, towel, or similar material to wipe up spills. Paper towels work well, too.

The Price of Good Soap

"Clean rooms, clean air, clean clothes, a clean body, and food hygiene—this is what is required. Cleanliness ought not in any way be seen as a luxury item only afforded the rich and affluent, but as a necessity for all people. Nobody can say that he cannot afford cleanliness. For this so little is needed: soap, water, and diligence."

THE MAGAZINE *HÄLSOVÄNNEN*, 1916 [FRIEND OF HEALTH 1916]

Soapmaking doesn't have to cost a lot of money, but it is a hobby with the potential to get very expensive. The cost depends on what kind of soap you want to make and what tools you want to use. The biggest villain is fragrance. Essential oils are concentrated plant extracts, difficult to distill, and can therefore be very costly to use. In addition, a large amount of essential oils is needed to give soap a long-lasting fragrance. It is fine to use perfume oils, which are somewhat cheaper and have a stronger scent. However, I'm not keen on artificial scents.

You can also choose to make a fragrance- and color-free natural soap, which is not expensive. I recommend making your first soap this way, and it will also have fewer manufacturing steps. I certainly understand, however, if you don't follow my advice, as I didn't either and ended up panic-stricken in a kitchen full of swirling activated charcoal when I made my first batch of soap.

Start out with homemade molds instead of buying expensive ones. I made my first soap batch in a thoroughly rinsed-out juice carton. Milk cartons, muffin tins, shoe boxes—lots of different containers work really well as soap molds, as long as you line them with parchment paper first to prevent the soap from sticking to the container. I have tried out many test soaps in empty tea carton molds, just the right size for small batches. That way, you use fewer ingredients and expensive additives; and if you're pleased with the result, you can use a larger mold next time. Single-size Pringle cartons are great for round soaps.

Color pigments are not expensive, and you only need to use a small amount. You can also use ingredients from the pantry to color your batter. On page 51 you'll see examples of natural color pigments and how they look when added to soap.

Some soapmakers use distilled water, i.e., pure water without any minerals or microorganisms. This is preferable if your water is hard with a lot of magnesium and calcium ions. If there are a lot of minerals or other impurities, the soap might feel slimy or the lather substandard. The soap can also become discolored, turn rancid, or create deposits in the sink when you use it. If you only make a small soap batch for yourself, try your tap water first to see how it works for soapmaking. Some soapmakers even use seawater. I've used both soft tap water and distilled water and have not noticed any discernible difference between them. Distilled water is sold quite inexpensively at most stores.

There are loads of different oils to choose from. Most important is the characteristic of the oil and how the soap composition turns out when different oils are mixed. If you use the right mixture, it really doesn't matter if the oil is an exclusive one or a common one like canola since the oils go through the same saponification process. Read more about this on page 37, and more about different oils and fatty acids on page 35.

If you decide soapmaking is for you, I suggest investing in larger amounts of essential oils, since they are often cheaper when bought in larger amounts.

Make a simple soap from coconut oil or coconut and olive oil if you want soapmaking to be as economical as possible. I do recommend that you try this the first time. That way you only need the bare minimum of ingredients: sodium hydroxide, water, and one or two oils. Such soap, without added colors or scents, and made with coconut oil that you buy in your local grocery store, will be both great and inexpensive.

KAUSTIK
SODA

CAUSTIC SODA
SODA KAUSTYCZN
KAUSTINEN SOOD

STARKT FRÄTANDE.
FÖR AVLUTNING, RENGÖRING
OCH AVLOPPSRENSNING.

750 g

Lye & Safety

"This is lye. The crucial ingredient." TYLER DURDEN, *FIGHT CLUB*

Lye (sodium hydroxide) is used widely in soapmaking. Lye is a strong base, so finished soap made with lye yields a high pH value, between 8 and 11. The skin's protective barrier, known as the stratum corneum, normally has a pH value between 4 and 6.

It is not problematic that handmade soap has a higher pH value because the soap will be rinsed off. Our skin is extremely fast at restoring pH balance, just 15 minutes on healthy skin.

Lye is sold in different forms like larger pellets, microbeads, and flakes. If the humidity level is low in your house (during the winter, for example), microbeads might fly around in the container due to static electricity. To avoid this, use larger pellets or flakes instead. That said, static electricity is more of a problem if using a plastic jug. Try using a stainless steel jug instead, or place a coffee filter in the jug before measuring the lye.

Lye needs to be kept in a jar with a tight-fitting lid because it attracts moisture and carbon dioxide from the air. Keep the jar well out of reach of children and any pets.

ALWAYS USE SAFETY EQUIPMENT WHEN YOU HANDLE LYE!

The bare minimum would be protective gloves and safety goggles and preferably a long-sleeved sweater, too. Eyeglasses will usually be sufficient, unless the frames are so small that the glasses don't cover the whole eye area. Mouth protection is good to avoid breathing in the fumes that are produced when you mix sodium hydroxide and water. An apron or some form of protective clothing is also practical because lye and soap batter mixture have a tendency to splatter.

Lye in water

Sodium hydroxide should always be poured into water, not the reverse. Don't mix lye in a glass container, even if it is laboratory glass. Lye reacts slowly in glass but will eventually damage the glass. The glass may break and you'll end up with lye everywhere. Lye also reacts with aluminum, so aluminum should never be used in the saponification process. Test your container with a magnet. If it stays put, it is stainless steel, but if it falls off, well, it is aluminum or something else. Only use safe plastic or stainless steel containers when making soap.

Vinegar

Tyler Durden, Brad Pitt's character in *Fight Club*, is correct when he says that vinegar neutralizes lye. Vinegar can be used directly on tools and other surfaces, but don't use it directly on the skin like they do in the film, because it causes an exothermic reaction that will aggravate a burn.

Rinse immediately with plenty of water if your skin has been in contact with lye. Use only water, nothing else! Rinse immediately, even if you don't feel burning or any other reaction. Sometimes the burn doesn't show or you don't feel it immediately, so it is imperative to rinse straight away.

DO THIS IF YOU HAVE COME IN DIRECT CONTACT WITH LYE:

INGESTED: Quickly rinse out your mouth and drink water. Do not try to induce vomiting. Go to the ER immediately.

IN THE EYES: Rinse eye(s) with running water for at least 15 minutes. Go to the ER and keep rinsing the eye(s) during transport to the ER.

ON THE SKIN: Rinse immediately with running water for at least 15 minutes. Wash the skin with soap and water. Change out of spotted clothes. Go to the ER if you notice skin irritation or burning.

Oils & Butters

Building blocks

Vegetable oils are triglycerides. They are built from three fatty acid molecules and one glycerol molecule.

Different oils are built from different oil molecule combinations. The fatty acids themselves have different characteristics that affect an oil's characteristics and feel, or how the soap turns out. Fatty acids are separated into saturated and unsaturated fats. The unsaturated fats are separated into monounsaturated and polyunsaturated fats.

The function of fatty acids is to give oils oily, dehydrating, emollient, and moisturizing characteristics. It is very important to find a good combination and balance of fatty acids. There are hundreds of fatty acids, but we only have to concentrate on eight of them.

The saturated fatty acids: Myristic acid, palmitic acid, stearic acid, and lauric acid primarily help soap trace and saponify faster. They make the soap hard and foamy and extend its shelf life.

The unsaturated fatty acids: Linoleic acids (omega 6), linolenic acid (omega 3), ricinoleic acid, and oleic acid (omega 9) slow down trace and are slower to saponify. They are softer and also make the soap softer, slower to harden, and they create a creamier lather. Ricinoleic acid extends a soap's shelf life and gives more stable foam and longer-lasting bubbles.

To get a great soap, you'll want a 40:60 ratio of saturated and unsaturated fats (40 percent hard oils/butters and 60 percent liquid oils).

LET'S DIVE FURTHER INTO FATTY ACIDS

Lauric, myristic, palmitic, and stearic acids are the saturated fats in soap that have an effect on soap hardness. These acids are found in oils that stay relatively hard at room temperature. Lauric and myristic fatty acids affect a soap's cleansing properties. The higher the concentration of these fatty acids, the more cleansing and dehydrating the soap. For normal skin, the total of these fatty acids should not exceed 10 to 22 percent of a recipe's fat content. If the recipe holds a higher amount of these acids, superfat needs to be increased to compensate for the acids' dehydrating effect. Someone with very sensitive skin might need a soap made without lauric and myristic acid.

Palmitic and stearic fatty acids affect a soap's shelf life. High levels of these fatty acids make a longer-lasting soap because they produce soap molecules that don't dissolve easily. However, the soap will lather less if there is an overabundance of these fatty acids. Palmitic and stearic fatty acids are found in harder kinds of butters. Use a total of 13 to 35 percent of these acids in soap for good firmness and durability.

Unsaturated oleic, linoleic, and linolenic acids affect a soap's emollient properties and their presence makes the soap dissolve easier. Oleic acid produces a creamier lather. Too much oleic acid, like in an olive oil–based soap, can give the soap's foam a slimy feel. Without affecting the feel of the lather, use a total of 32 to 50 percent of oleic acid in soap. Linolenic and linoleic fatty acids increase the risk for rancidity and developing dreaded orange spots (see page 127). Don't use more than a total of 15 percent of these fatty acids in a soap recipe.

Unsaponifiables

Vegetable oils contain substances called unsaponifiables. These substances may be antioxidants, vitamins, or phytosterols and they are not saponified during the soapmaking process. Squalane, one such unsaponifiable, is mostly extracted from olive oil, used in skin care, and currently very trendy.

Unsaponifiables can give soap various desired qualities. How many unsaponifiables to use in an oil can vary from one batch to the next. There is an ongoing discussion within the soapmaking community whether certain substances survive the saponification process or not. Save your expensive oils for lotions, or perhaps use them in a hot process soap where you have more control over which oil will be the superfat.

Longevity

Bacteria and mold don't grow in oil, but oil can still go rancid, which happens with oxidation. You can often tell a rancid oil by its smell, but don't confuse it with the particular smell of certain cold-pressed oils. Oils containing a lot of saturated fatty acids have a longer shelf life, while oils with a lot of polyunsaturated fatty acids have a shorter shelf life.

The freshness of your oils affects a soap's shelf life. You face greater risk of your soap going rancid if you use old oil or oil nearing its best-by date. Rancid soap smells unpleasant and will be slimy. It is best to just throw it out.

Store your oils in tightly capped bottles or jars in a dark and cool place. Unopened bottles can be stored in the refrigerator; the oil might turn turbid and opaque, but it won't affect the oil's properties.

Saponification value

Each oil has a saponification value. Several factors like harvest, batch, air humidity, and so on make an oil's saponification value vary. Each oil has a saponification safety margin to make sure that there is never any leftover lye in the finished soap. Thanks to available soap calculators, you don't have to keep these numbers in your head. There are also ready-made charts where the saponification value is already converted to show how much sodium hydroxide is needed for saponification of different oils. Olive oil's saponification value, for example, is 0.134, which means that you'll need 0.134 grams of sodium hydroxide to saponify 1 gram of olive oil.

It is very important to remember that you can't replace an oil in a recipe without reformulating the recipe because the saponification value changes with the oil used. Some oils have the same saponification value, so they are interchangeable, but get into the habit of recalculating your recipe (see page 64) when you change oils. If you suddenly run out of the specified oil for a recipe you can't just make up the difference with any other oil. To avoid running short, it is best to measure the exact oil amount in advance.

Oils for soapmaking

COLD PRESSED, REFINED & DEODORIZED

Oils are extracted and treated in several ways. Cold pressed oil has been extracted through a gentle process that, in order to preserve antioxidants and vitamins, is not heated past 95°F (35°C). This process requires more seeds to get enough oil, as not all oil is extracted from the seeds, making cold pressed oil more expensive as a result. Cold pressed oils are often darker and oxidize faster.

Refined oil is expressed with a warm process where some vitamins and other substances are lost. The oil is more neutral in color, has less flavor, and is cheaper. It is common to enrich refined oil with vitamin E to give it a longer shelf life.

Deodorized oil is treated with steam to remove flavor and scent. Coconut and shea butter exist in deodorized versions, as they sometimes have strong odors we want to avoid.

All of these oils are suitable for saponification. Refined oil might be preferable due to its extended shelf life and lower cost.

AVOCADO OIL. A popular nutritious oil. May make soap soft, so don't use more than 20 percent avocado oil in a soap recipe, and combine it with solid oils and butters. Avocado oil contains high levels of oleic acid. It also contains a higher amount of unsaponifiables, among them several vitamins. This oil is greenish-yellow and the color does affect the soap color.

HEMP SEED OIL. This dark green oil is suitable for facial soaps and shampoos. These soaps will be moisturizing and lather very well. Hemp oil contains a lot of linoleic acid. Add up to 15 percent to a recipe.

JOJOBA SEED OIL. Many soapmakers like this specialty oil. The advantage of jojoba oil is that it can be used in facial soaps for all skin types. This is more of a strongly yellow liquid wax than an oil. Jojoba seed oil consists largely of gadoleic acid, which is naturally present in our skin. Use up to 10 percent of this oil in a recipe.

COCOA BUTTER. I love the smell of cocoa butter but it is a light golden brown, so you should avoid it if you want a perfectly white soap. Cocoa butter contains stearic, palmitic, and oleic acids. It has a low content of unsaponifiables, which is preferable in a shampoo. Use a maximum of 15 to 18 percent in your recipe.

COCONUT OIL. Coconut oil is becoming increasingly popular for different applications. It's great for soapmaking, as it makes a hard soap with good cleansing properties. Some people don't like the coconut aroma, but you can get deodorized coconut oil without scent or flavor. Use up to 25 to 30 percent in recipes. The more coconut oil used, the more cleansing and dehydrating the soap. If you have sensitive skin, use less than 20 percent in the recipe, or increase the superfat. Coconut oil can be used in larger amounts (up to 100 percent) for specialty products like coconut soap, salt soap, and bodywash.

LAUREL OIL. This oil has a strong odor that is not popular with everybody. Its color is dark green, which affects the finished soap's color. Laurel oil contains oleic, linoleic, laurel, and palmitic acids, and 2 to 3 percent unsaponifiables, including essential oil.

FLAXSEED OIL. From this oil you can make flax soap, a useful cleaning product. The oil contains a large amount of linolenic acid. It is quite unnecessary to use this oil in cold process soap, so restrict it to 5 percent if you want to add some.

ALMOND OIL. Almond oil is slightly less yellow than canola oil, so some soapmakers prefer to use this in place of canola oil. Almond oil contains mostly oleic and linoleic acid. Use up to 15 to 20 percent in your recipe.

MANGO BUTTER. This specialty butter is more expensive and difficult to find compared to other oils. Still, mango butter appears often in soapmaking because it produces a hard soap with a super lather. This butter contains a lot of stearic and oleic acid. Use up to 30 percent in a recipe.

OLIVE OIL. Olive oil is a very common and good basic oil in hard soap. It's moisturizing and can be used on its own, but it needs a long curing period. Olive oil gives soap a greenish yellowy tint. I prefer refined olive oil, which is lighter in color and won't affect the finished soap's color quite as much. Olive oil contains a lot of monounsaturated oleic acid (omega-9). It also has linoleic and palmitic acid.

PALM OIL. Palm oil is commonly found in soapmaking because it produces a soap that is both hard and mild. However, it is not sustainable due to the deforestation of rain forests in favor of palm oil plantations. Buy only organic oil if you want to use palm oil. None of the recipes in this book use palm oil.

CANOLA OIL. Canola oil is very yellow, which also turns the soap yellowish. Use 15 to 20 percent in your recipe.

CASTOR OIL. Castor oil is a specialty oil and the only one that contains ricinoleic acid. This stable and viscous oil is slow to oxidize. It is considered a booster oil in soap, as it boosts and stabilizes other oils containing lauric and myristic acid. Castor oil is mostly colorless. It speeds up trace. Don't use too much castor oil because it will make the soap sticky. Five to 10 percent is sufficient.

SHEA BUTTER. I find shea to be an excellent butter and I use it very often in my soaps. It is also good for skin care. Shea butter contains up to 5 percent unsaponifiables, which is more than many other fats. Nondeodorized shea butter will have a characteristically smoky scent that disappears during saponification. Depending on the recipe, use 15 to 20 percent shea butter.

SUNFLOWER OIL. Sunflower oil, unfortunately, has a large amount of linoleic acid, which gives it a short and unstable shelf life. Sunflower oil increases the risk of the soap turning rancid. There is a specialty sunflower oil with a larger oleic acid content that is better for soapmaking, but it is of course more expensive. Don't use more than 15 percent sunflower oil in a recipe.

WAX. If you want a harder soap, use wax like beeswax, soy wax, or rice wax. Use between 1 and 3 percent in the recipe.

A few quick pointers (great if they are followed but it's entirely up to you):
Keep a ratio of 40:60 between hard and liquid oils. Forty percent hard oils/saturated fatty acids, 60 percent liquid oils/unsaturated fatty acids.

Water

You'll need water to mix lye with oil(s) but it's up to you how much water you want in your recipe. Follow any of these three steps to calculate the amount of water needed:

- Percentage of an oil's weight
- Lye concentration
- Relationship between water and lye in the soap batter

Most soap calculators have a default setting with the water amount at 38 percent of an oil's weight. It is preset for hot process soap but often needs to be changed for cold process, as this is far too much water. I recommend calculating water using the lye concentration because it is a constant number in all recipes, whereas oil weights vary depending on specific oils used.

When you change the lye concentration in a soap calculator, it is only the amount of water, rather than the amount of lye, that changes. The amount of lye required for a specific recipe depends on which oils and the amount of these oils the recipe contains.

Using less water than the preset amount in a soap calculator is called water reduction. This can be a good way to influence a soap batter's trace and cure time. It also affects how likely it is for soap batter to gel, the risk for glycerin floods, soap ash, and other things. Overall, water reduction can be favorable, as there is really no reason to have a lot of water in your soap batter.

TWENTY-EIGHT PERCENT is the lowest recommended lye concentration for soapmaking. This is a ratio of slightly over 2.5:1 for water to lye, which is an awful lot of water. It provides extended time for making complicated swirls as the soap batter trace is slower. It also increases the chance (or risk, depending on the result you're looking for) of the soap batter starting to gel. The resulting soap will be very soft, will take a long time to harden, and needs long curing. The risk for various cosmetic defects in the soap, like soap ash and glycerin flooding, is increased.

THIRTY-THREE TO 35 PERCENT lye concentration is more commonly used. The ratio is about 2:1 between water and lye, i.e., nearly double water to lye. That is still a lot of water that needs to evaporate from the soap, and the risk for soap ash and other defects is great, but it gives you more time to work with patterns and an increased chance for gelling. This amount of water is good for soap that hardens quickly like 100 percent coconut soap.

FORTY PERCENT lye concentration is good for soaps with a large number of liquid oils, like 100 percent olive oil soap. Less water reduces the risk for glycerin floods in the soap and soap ash. The soap needs shorter curing time. Forty percent has a lye concentration ratio of 1.5:1 water to lye. This is my preferred lye concentration.

FIFTY PERCENT lye concentration is the highest lye concentration to use in soapmaking. This means a ratio of 1:1, i.e., equal amounts lye as water in the recipe. For the sodium hydroxide to dissolve properly, you need to have the same amount of water as lye. Many prefer to use a slightly lower lye concentration to be on the safe side. I strongly recommend that you do this.

Many soapmakers prefer to use distilled water to avoid possible metal residue. However, tap water often works just as well, especially if your water is soft. You can also use salt water or sea water if you like. Salt makes for a harder and whiter soap.

Additives

The acronym PPO (per pound of oils) is used in soapmaking to describe color pigments, plant extracts, and other additives. PPO is often rounded to 450 grams, but to make the recipes clearer in this book, I've rounded up to 500 grams.

Adding fragrance

"Osiris (God of the Afterlife) is the body of the plants, Nefertum (God of Divine Scents & Healing) is the soul of the plants, the plants purified. The divine perfume belongs to Nefertum, living forever."

HYMN TO NEFERTUM, EIGHTEENTH DYNASTY

ESSENTIAL OILS

It's good to combine essential oils that have a top, middle, and base note to get a longer lasting scent. You can assume, in principle, that the light fresh scents are top notes and don't last as long. The heavier scents are base notes and last the longest. A guideline to follow in scent mixing would be 30 percent top note, 50 percent middle note, and 20 percent base note.

If you are using ½ ounce (15 grams) essential oil in your recipe, take 0.159 ounce (4.5 grams) orange, 0.265 ounce (7.5 grams) lavender, and 0.106 ounce (3 grams) patchouli.

Of course, it's not necessary for you to use three different oils. You can use one, two, or five. It's not written in stone that you have to have a top, middle, and base note, but using the note system makes for a livelier scent that lasts longer. If you use just top notes, like citrus, remember that the scent might not last as long because top notes are transient.

I suggest mixing a small amount of essential oils in advance to make sure that you will like a scent mix. For example, take a total of 10 drops (100 percent), and divide the drops into different percentages. Place a drop of your mix on a round cotton pad, wait a while, then take a whiff.

It can be difficult for soap to retain a scent, so I usually anchor scents in advance in 1 teaspoon kaolinite clay, also called China clay, by measuring out the essential oils and mixing them with the clay. This mix can easily rest a few hours before soapmaking.

You can also anchor scents in cornstarch, which gives the soap a smooth texture. Use up to ½ tablespoon starch to 1 pound (500 grams) oils and mix the starch and essential oils together.

Arrowroot and all-purpose flour are good alternatives to cornstarch.

Called the queen of scents, it's not strange that lavender is perhaps the most popular essential oil. I recommend lavender if you're only choosing one essential oil! It works on its own as well as with any scent you want.

Citrus is a tricky one and doesn't hold up in soap. Good alternatives to citrus are *Litsea cubeba*, lemongrass, and citronella because they have more staying power. Cinnamon is a wonderful scent but it can irritate sensitive skin, so go easy. Cinnamon leaf oil is a milder alternative. Cloves can also irritate skin, so use it only in small quantities. Check out the next page and eocalc.com for tips on nice scent mixes and safe amounts of essential oils to use in soap.

Examples of scent combinations

2 OILS

- Orange 70 percent, patchouli 30 percent
- Lavender 50 percent, *Litsea cubeba* 50 percent
- Lavender 80 percent, vetiver 20 percent
- Cedar 60 percent, juniper 40 percent
- Lemongrass 70 percent, clary sage 30 percent
- Palmarosa 70 percent, patchouli 30 percent

3 OILS

- Pine needles 40 percent, juniper 30 percent, cypress 30 percent
- Lavender 40 percent, sage 40 percent, frankincense 20 percent
- Bergamot 50 percent, patchouli 25 percent, cedar 25 percent
- Lavender 40 percent, tea tree 30 percent, *Litsea cubeba* 30 percent
- Orange 50 percent, vetiver 30 percent, patchouli 20 percent
- Orange 50 percent, ylang-ylang 30 percent, sage 20 percent
- Frankincense 40 percent, bergamot 30 percent, rose geranium 30 percent

FAKE VERSION OF KYPHI. Kyphi was the name of Ancient Egypt's most famous perfume. The recipe is complicated and there are three versions engraved on old Egyptian temples. You can make a fake version: Myrrh 40 percent, juniper 40 percent, and cinnamon 20 percent.

4 OILS

- Bergamot 35 percent, orange 35 percent, peppermint 20 percent, *Litsea cubeba* 10 percent
- Lavender 50 percent, sage 20 percent, rosemary 20 percent, juniper 10 percent
- Lavender 40 percent, bergamot 30 percent, Amyris 20 percent, geranium 10 percent

- Orange 40 percent, clove 20 percent, cinnamon 20 percent, anise 20 percent

5 OILS
- Lemon 20 percent, eucalyptus 20 percent, peppermint 20 percent, rosemary 20 percent, lavender 20 percent
- Lavender 50 percent, clary sage 20 percent, orange 10 percent, patchouli 10 percent, cedar 10 percent

THIEVES' MIXTURE. Legend has it, thieving seamen protected themselves from the Black Death when plundering corpses of valuables, by using these antibacterial essential oils. They are supposed to have used garlic and vinegar, too, but that's hardly attractive in soap: Clove 20 percent, lemon 20 percent, cinnamon 20 percent, eucalyptus 20 percent, and rosemary 20 percent.

AQUA MIRABILIS. The original recipe for the historical Eau de Cologne is clouded in secrecy, but here is a copycat recipe to use in soap: Grapefruit 20 percent, bergamot 20 percent, neroli (bitter orange) 20 percent, rosemary 20 percent, and lavender 20 percent.

THE QUEEN OF HUNGARY'S WATER/EAU DE LA REINE DE HONGARY. One of the first modern perfumes was made in the 1370s by order of the queen of Hungary to help alleviate her headaches. The mixture was primarily a rosemary tincture, later developed to contain several scents. Make a simplified version of this scent mix: Rosemary 30 percent, lemon verbena (or other citrus scent) 20 percent, rose or lavender 20 percent, sage 20 percent, and orange 10 percent.

FRAGRANCE OILS
Fragrance oils, i.e., synthetically produced scents, are perfectly fine to use in soap, as long as you don't mind artificial scents. Fragrance oils are cheaper

than essential oils and you can often buy ready-made mixes so don't have to make your own. I usually prefer to use essential oils, but some scents, like vanilla, are difficult to find as an essential oil, so fragrance oils are sometimes necessary. Many scents, like chocolate, don't even exist as essential oils because they are impossible to extract. You'll find them as fragrance oils.

Some essential oils and fragrance oils will color the soap. As a rule, a dark essential oil will color the soap toward the dark end of the spectrum, so it is best to use pale essential oils if your goal is to create as white a soap as possible. Fragrance oils that contain vanilla will make the soap turn brown when it cures. You can use this to your advantage by using a brown design.

Coloring

Coloring soap can be done in several ways, either using natural or synthetic colors. The most common ways are to use mica pigment, oxides, and natural powders.

MICA PIGMENT

Mica is a mineral that is extracted in mines and can also be produced synthetically. Due to many alarming reports about child labor use in mica extraction, many mica users now turn to synthetic mica, which is not a natural mineral.

If you want to use natural mica, make sure that the powder you buy is ethically sourced. Use approximately 1 teaspoon mica powder to 1 pound (500 grams) oil.

MINERAL PIGMENTS

Apart from mica, oxide and ultramarine mineral pigments can be used as soap colorants. Often all that's needed is a small amount of powder to produce lots of color, so start with ½ teaspoon to 1 pound (500 grams) water or oil. Mix the powder thoroughly with the water or oil before adding it to soap batter to avoid the pigments bleeding when you cut the soap.

Ultramarines mix well with water, but oxide pigments need oil because they don't mix with water.

TITANIUM DIOXIDE

Titanium dioxide (titanium white) is a completely white mineral, but it isn't regarded as a natural pigment because it needs to be refined. Titanium dioxide with nanoparticles is suspected of being carcinogenic but titanium dioxide without nanoparticles is fine to use in soap products. Use about 1 teaspoon titanium dioxide per 1 pound (500 grams) oil. Mix 1 teaspoon titanium dioxide in 1 tablespoon water or oil in advance of use. If the titanium dioxide doesn't dissolve properly, it might cause white spots in the soap.

I premix a large quantity in a plastic tub so I don't have to mix a new batch for each use. Remember, if you premix, you will need 1 tablespoon of the mix per 1 pound (500 grams) soap (1 teaspoon titanium dioxide per 1 tablespoon oil).

NATURAL COLORANTS

There are many natural colorants you can use to add color to soap. You probably already have some good ones in your pantry. These are mixed with the soap batter in various ways, either through mixing the color into the lye, adding the color at trace, or making an extract in oil.

Some colorants replace the water in a soap recipe. As a guideline, start with 1 teaspoon powder per 1 pound (500 grams) oils. The amount of colorant used will of course affect the strength of the soap's final color. Too much colorant can lead to the soap bleeding a lot of color when used, and it can also affect the consistency of the soap. One teaspoon is a good starting point.

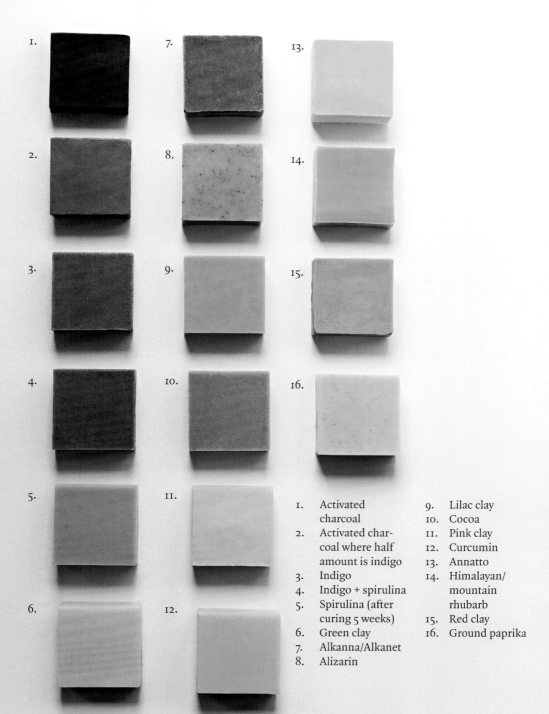

1. Activated charcoal
2. Activated charcoal where half amount is indigo
3. Indigo
4. Indigo + spirulina
5. Spirulina (after curing 5 weeks)
6. Green clay
7. Alkanna/Alkanet
8. Alizarin
9. Lilac clay
10. Cocoa
11. Pink clay
12. Curcumin
13. Annatto
14. Himalayan/ mountain rhubarb
15. Red clay
16. Ground paprika

CLAYS—Dissolve in some water and add prior to or at trace. You can also mix the clays with essential oils.

GROUND PAPRIKA—Prepare an oil extract. You can also add the powder directly to the soap batter, but it will show up as dots.

SPIRULINA—Dissolve in some lukewarm to warm water and add prior to or at trace.

COCOA—Dissolve it with oil or water and add prior to or at trace. Don't use more than ⅙ ounce (5 grams) per 1 pound (500 grams) of oils.

CURCUMIN—Dissolve with oil or water and add prior to or at trace.

ACTIVATED CHARCOAL—You can add this directly to the soap batter, but it absorbs water, so I recommend dissolving it in some water beforehand.

ALKANNA/ALKANET—Prepare an oil extract. A good way is to use an oil from the recipe, such as olive oil, and make an extract using the whole amount.

ALIZARIN—Prepare an oil extract or infuse in water and strain. You can add it straight to the soap batter but it will cause small dots to appear.

HIMALAYAN (MOUNTAIN) RHUBARB—Prepare an oil extract.

ANNATTO—Prepare an oil extract.

CARROT JUICE—Replace the recipe's water with this. You can replace all or just part of the water.

COFFEE—Replace the water with this.

BEER—Replace the water with this.

INDIGO—Indigo is extremely potent so use less than ½ teaspoon per 1 pound (500 grams) of oil. You can make an oil extract or dissolve it in water before you add the sodium hydroxide.

BOTANICAL EXTRACTS

Oil extracts, made by mixing plant matter or powder with oil, can produce great colors to add to your soap batter.

There are several ways to make botanical oil extracts. Make them from dried plants, herbs, or ground powders. The plants won't turn moldy in the oil as long as they are completely dry.

I prefer to make extracts in pale olive oil because it is a good clean oil. Most soap recipes use a good deal of olive oil, which increases the uptake of color and various nourishing substances in the soap.

SLOW METHOD. Fill a glass jar to the brim with dried plants or calculate the amount of plant powder you need for the recipe and place that in the jar. Fill the jar with olive oil and keep it at room temperature but out of direct sunlight. Let the jar rest for 3 to 4 weeks, giving it a shake now and then.

STILL SLOW BUT SLIGHTLY QUICKER METHOD. Fill the jar the same way as above but place the jar in a window. If there is direct sunlight, place the jar in a brown paper bag. (Direct sunlight makes the oil oxidize quickly, turning it rancid.) The extract will be ready in about 2 weeks because of the extra warmth.

QUICK METHOD. You can use this method if you have a slow cooker. This cookware is also handy it you want to try hot process soap or make a re-batch (see page 131). In a slow cooker, place the dried plant matter or powder and pour oil over. Set it on lowest heat setting for 1 hour. Turn off the heat and let the mixture rest until the next day. Then, repeat the procedure at lowest setting for 1 hour. Repeat this process for 3 days, and your extract is ready.

SUPER QUICK METHOD. Well, 1 to 2 hours might not be super quick by today's standards, but this is the quick fix for plant extracts. Using a double boiler or bain marie, fill some water in the bottom pan and make sure the water doesn't touch the heatproof pan above.

Place the dried plant matter in a glass jar and pour over the oil, then place the glass jar in the heatproof pan.

Bring the water to a boil and let it simmer about 1 to 2 hours. Keep an eye on the water so it doesn't completely evaporate. It's best to use a thermometer to make sure the extract doesn't overheat—many good plant and herb substances are lost if they are heated above 140°F (60°C).

Strain the extract when you are ready to use it. Powder has a tendency to really stick to the bottom of the jar—if that happens there is no need to strain. However, if you want to make absolutely sure that larger grains don't end up in your soap, pour the extract through a fine mesh strainer.

GELLING & COLOR

Gelling typically makes soap colors deeper, but the shades may vary in intensity. A white soap gets whiter by not gelling.

ACTIVATED CHARCOAL

Activated charcoal is popular in the beauty and health industry, primarily because of its cleansing properties. It attracts dirt, chemicals, bacteria, and other nasties. It's said that just 1 teaspoon of spilled activated charcoal covers the area of a soccer field. Whether this is true or not, it is certain that even the tiniest amount seems to end up just about everywhere.

Depending on the amount used, activated charcoal can produce anything from a pale gray to black soap. To avoid clumps, mix the charcoal with some oil before you add it to the soap batter. How black the soap turns out depends on the product manufacturer, but use approximately 2 teaspoons activated charcoal per 1 pound (500 grams) of oil to get black, and less for shades of gray.

WHITE SOAP

". . . wash me, and I shall be whiter than snow." PSALM 51:7

I would guess that 95 percent of all people think of white soap when we mention soap. The feeling that soap ought to be white is because, after all, white represents something that is clean. White soaps are wonderful but not quite as easy to achieve as you'd think.

There are several ways to affect soap's whiteness. You can use titanium dioxide (titanium white) and kaolin clay to make soap white. Zinc oxide will make the soap paler rather than truly white. A 100 percent coconut soap will be white but also somewhat transparent. You can also use salt water in your recipe to make the soap whiter. One deciding factor of soap color is of course the color of the oils. If you use greenish-yellow extra virgin olive oil, the color will affect the soap, making it very difficult to get a completely white soap.

Dairy products, honey, or artificial fragrances containing vanilla will turn the soap color brownish. Use the palest oils possible if you want a truly white soap.

Other additives

EXFOLIANT SCRUB

Exfoliant scrubs remove coarse dirt when you wash your hands and also remove dead skin cells when you wash your body. A common mistake made by novice soapmakers is adding too much of an exfoliating substance to soap. This makes the soap very scratchy and only suitable for treating coarse heel skin. Use less of an exfoliating substance than you think is needed.

Some good exfoliants for soap: used coffee grounds (dried), ground oats, poppy seeds, tea leaves (dried), salt, and finely ground lemon rinds.

With the exception of marigolds and cornflower, dried flowers and leaves, unfortunately, don't keep their color in soap. Most oxidize from the lye and turn brown. Even if you're itching to mix lavender flowers in the soap, please don't. The flowers will turn brown and look like mouse droppings.

CLAYS

Clay helps bind the scent in soap, and it also gives the soap a softer feel. Depending on which clay you use, it can also give the soap a very nice and natural color.

A good starting point is to use 1 teaspoon clay per 1 pound (500 grams) of oil. Mix 1 teaspoon clay with 1 tablespoon water. If you have time and patience, do this a few hours before you're going to use it so that the clay has time to absorb the water before you mix it into the soap batter.

Don't mix in any water if you mix the clay with essential oils. The clay accelerates trace somewhat—the more clay, the quicker the trace.

SODIUM LACTATE

Sodium lactate is used to get a harder soap. Unlike salt, sodium lactate produces better lather. It is mixed into the lye once the lye has cooled to 114.8°F (46°C) or lower. Use 1 to 3 percent of the oils' weight. I usually use 1½ teaspoons (approximately ¼ ounce/7.5 grams) per 1 pound (500 grams) of oils. This works out to 1.6 percent sodium lactate. You don't need to add salt if you use sodium lactate, and vice versa.

SALT

Salt is an excellent ingredient for harder soap. Use common table salt without iodine, sea salt, or Himalayan salt. Avoid salt with a high content of minerals, such as Dead Sea salt.

Use 1 teaspoon salt per 1 pound (500 grams) of oils to get a harder soap.

Mix salt with water before you add the sodium hydroxide. A tip is to add sugar to the recipe, as salt inhibits lather. You don't need to add salt if you use sodium lactate, and vice versa.

SUGAR

Sugar provides stable and longer lasting bubbles and accelerates trace. Be careful when using lots of sugar or other sugary ingredients because the batter gets very hot.

Use either table sugar or confectioners' sugar. Confectioners' sugar contains a tiny amount of potato starch to prevent clumping, and starch is a useful additive in soap. It is said that confectioners' sugar produces a creamier lather than table sugar but I have not noticed any difference.

HONEY

Honey contains lots of dextrose and fructose, which create a rich and sustained lather.

Honey accelerates trace, making the soap batter very warm, so there's a risk of the soap batter burning if you use a lot of honey (the batter will get dark and start to smell not so great). To lessen the risk of burnt batter, add honey as a last step before you pour the soap into the mold. One to 2 teaspoons per 1 pound (500 grams) of oils is a good starting point. Honey needs to be dissolved in some water before it is added. Make sure the honey is mixed thoroughly into the batter.

CITRIC ACID

Citric acid can be used in soap to avoid soap scum, that lime deposit which can be seen in bathtubs and on shower walls and is incredibly difficult to remove. The tendency for soap scum to develop is greater if your water is hard and contains calcium and magnesium. Citric acid is sour but it doesn't interfere with a soap's pH.

Citric acid reacts with sodium hydroxide to create trisodium citrate—called a chelate. A chelate is a chemical that binds ions so that they can't bind to the soap molecules. This leads to less risk of the soap's oils turning rancid; in effect, the soap has a longer shelf life and there is less risk for soap scum build-up.

Citric acid works best at between 0.5 to 2 percent of the oils' weight. Citric acid neutralizes sodium hydroxide, so the superfat in the soap increases. If you want to control the superfat, add extra sodium hydroxide according to this formula when you mix lye: ⅕ ounce (6 grams) extra sodium hydroxide per ⅓ ounce (10 grams) citric acid.

STARCH

Cornstarch is probably the most commonly used starch by soapmakers. Starch protects against formation of soap scum and makes soap texture smooth. You can also use cornstarch to anchor scents. Use up to ½ tablespoon cornstarch per 1 pound (500 grams) of oils.

Sorbitol is synthetically extracted from starch and can be used in soap to achieve a more abundant and stable lather.

Oats, a popular soap ingredient, are also starchy.

OATS

Oats can be added to soap in different formats: oat oil, colloidal oatmeal, whole oats, ground oats/oatmeal, or oat milk. Colloidal oats are different from oatmeal. They're blended into an extra fine powder to allow the skin to absorb the substances in the oat.

It is better and also very simple to make your own oat milk (see page 110).

It might be tempting to add whole oats for an exfoliating effect, but it could end up a real mess, so I recommend grinding the oats first.

MILK

Primarily goat, oat, and coconut milk are popular in soapmaking. They produce a good lather and have a soothing effect. Just make sure your milk doesn't contain a lot of additives that you wouldn't want on your skin. Some plant-based milks, like oat and almond, are better made at home.

Decorate the soap

Some soapmakers create the most fantastic soap tops with the help of a variety of swirls and added decorations. Popular organic materials good for decorating soap are: coffee beans and ground coffee, dried jasmine, marigolds and daisies, dried orange slices, mustard seeds, dried sage leaves, poppy seeds, oats, spices, tea leaves, Himalayan salt, dried rose buds or leaves, dried berries, and seeds.

You can also decorate soap tops with color pigment or natural powder. Sift pigment over the whole soap once you've poured it into the mold or mix pigment with rubbing alcohol and, once the soap has hardened, paint this on the soap with a brush.

Use tweezers if you want to place coffee beans, for example, because it's easy to disturb the soap with your gloved fingers.

[PART 2]
Practice

Create a Recipe

Mathematical calculation is one of the drawbacks to soapmaking. For those of us whose favorite subject in high school wasn't the Pythagorean theorem, this can be a real pain. You will have to deal with assorted calculations if you want to experiment with different shapes, colors, scents, and oils in soapmaking. Some things are okay to estimate, but amounts, percentages, and volumes must be calculated.

How to calculate the volume of a new mold

It is possible, in a nerdy I-love-math kind of way, to accurately calculate your homemade mold or a purchased mold if it's missing information about how much soap batter it can hold, but this is how a simpler calculation is done:

Multiply the length, width, and depth of the mold by 0.70. This number is the amount of oil the recipe requires.

To calculate a round mold: use pi (3.14) × radius × radius × depth of the mold × 0.70.

The number 0.70 is the accepted starting point but it depends, of course, on how much water you actually use in the recipe, and also on the weight and density of the oils. This number works well for most recipes, especially if you use a common lye concentration of around 35 to 38 percent. Keep extra molds handy in case you end up with too much soap batter.

Soap calculator

A soap calculator is the soapmaker's best friend. I, and many others, use the recipe calculator on SoapCalc (soapcalc.net), so I will be discussing just that one.

For a newbie using SoapCalc, it can be like trying to read data programming without having the slightest clue what it is. Don't panic at the sight of all the numbers, blocks, and buttons, because it's not quite as complicated as it first seems.

When you enter an oil, you'll see its fatty acid composition to the left in the "One" column. In the right-hand column to the left under "All," you'll see the values for the oil mixture you have already added to the recipe. The values for the oil mixture show the different properties the soap will have and the approximate range the value should stay within. This is just a guideline and not set in stone. For example, in the "Cleansing" row underneath the "One" column, the soap will still be cleansing even if the value is 0.

Some soap recipes will show strange numbers even though they are great soaps. I suggest experimenting and testing around these values because these values don't take into account different additives, how the soap is made, superfat, or curing time. Sodium lactate, salt, and other additives will produce a harder soap even if the value in the "Hardness" row under the "One" column shows a soft soap. Sugar will produce more bubbles even if the oil mixture's bubble value is low. The SoapCalc numbers are based solely on the fatty acids in the recipe.

VALUES

HARDNESS. Indicates the finished soap's hardness.

CLEANSING. This number can also be easy to misinterpret because soap is always cleansing but can be more or less rough on the skin. A high cleansing value can dry out the skin more than a low value.

CONDITION. This number can indicate a mild soap, but it doesn't take into account all the fatty acids that create a milder soap.

BUBBLY. How bubbly a soap's lather is indicates how rich the lather becomes from the fatty acid combination. Don't spend too much time on this column.

CREAMY. The lather's creaminess. Additives can affect the lather a lot.

IODINE VALUE. The lower the value, the harder the soap.

INS VALUE. is optimal around 160 but that is just a pointer.

You don't need to enter colorants or essential oils in the soap calculator because these are added in addition to the oils and lye in the recipe, even when they're diluted in water or oil.

At the bottom of SoapCalc's recipe calculator, you'll find links to more explanations and even a "Sort Oil List" where you can sort oil depending on fatty acids and other desired values.

Step-by-Step

Once you have read about the saponification process and acquired all the necessary tools and ingredients, it is time to create a soap recipe. You can begin with one of this book's recipes or create a whole new recipe of your own. The most important step, which I can't emphasize enough, is to always check your recipe in the soap calculator. Do this even for recipes from this book (if for no other reason than to learn how the soap calculator works and how the different numbers are supposed to look).

Prepare scent and additives.

1. Prepare everything you need

Once soapmaking has started, some ele-
ments of the process move along quickly.
Make sure everything you need is handy.
Get out your scales, oils, and sodium
hydroxide. You'll need additives, gloves,
safety glasses, tools, and a soap mold.
Keep the recipe handy while you work.
(I don't have a good memory for numbers
so I check the recipe for each measure,
sometimes several times.) If you need to
protect your work surface, put down some
kind of protective layer; paper towels or a
cloth to be able to wipe up spills immediately. If you are going to force gelling,
now's the time to set the oven to 150°F
(70°C) to 200°F (100°C).

2. Mix scent and colorant

If you use clay to anchor your soap's
scent(s), let the preparation stand a while.
Mix any color pigments, clays, or titanium
dioxide with oil or water.

Measure out sodium hydroxide.

Don protective gear.

3. Protective gear

Put on safety goggles and gloves.

4. Mix lye

Measure out the correct amount of water or ice cubes in a pitcher. In a second pitcher, measure sodium hydroxide. Always put these items in separate pitchers because it is easy to pour too much sodium hydroxide directly into the water. Don't forget, you should always pour sodium hydroxide into the water, never vice versa.

Carefully add the sodium hydroxide to the water and stir until completely dissolved. It might be slightly cloudy but that's okay. The mixture doesn't need to be completely transparent. Place the pitcher in a safe place that won't be disturbed.

Measure out the oils.

Mix lye and oils.

5. Melt and mix the oils

Using a microwave, you can melt the hard oils first, 30 seconds at a time, or heat in a saucepan on low, while keeping a close eye on it. You can also measure out all oils and melt them together.

Stir together the liquid oils and the melted fats. Mix in essential oils and colorants in this step if you want to.

6. Mix lye and oils

Pour the lye carefully into the oils. Use a sieve, if necessary, to remove small residue particles that might stick to the surface of the lye. Stir with a spatula. I often add color pigments in this step. If you are using more than one color in the soap, add the color pigments after mixing.

PRACTICE

Blend.

Pour soap mixture into the mold.

7. Blend

Position the immersion blender so that it is leaning away from the center of the mixture to allow eventual air bubbles to escape. Tap the blender lightly against the bottom of the pitcher to release any air bubbles that are trapped below the blender head.

Stir a few turns with the blender turned off. Turn on the blender and blend for 2 to 3 seconds. Stir the mixture again and check the surface for trace. Blend for another 2 to 3 seconds. Continue in this mode, resting and stirring and checking for trace. Different recipes trace at different speeds. Even the same recipe can trace at different speeds depending on various factors.

Stop blending when you've reached the desired trace—light, medium, or thick.

Never leave the immersion blender standing on its own in the mixing bowl, as the blender can fall, tipping the bowl over with the unsaponified caustic soap mixture.

8. Pour into a mold

Divide the soap mixture between different pitchers and add multiple colorants now if you want multicolored soap. Work quickly so the soap doesn't have time to thicken too much.

Guide the soap mixture down along the head of the spatula into the mold to avoid too many air pockets. Scrape out the pitcher with the spatula to get all the soap mixture.

Once the mold is filled, lift it a little and let it drop down or tap it on your work surface to remove existing air bubbles in the mixture. Do this several times. Decorate or make patterns on top.

Make pattern on top.

Cut the soap.

9. Insulation

Cover the soap mold with cardboard, plastic film, or something similar to prevent too much contact with oxygen. If you are going to oven-heat the soap, turn off the oven but leave the oven light on. Place the mold in the oven and leave it overnight. An alternative is to wrap the mold in a towel or other textile material to provide an even heat.

10. Cut up the soap

The time for soap to harden enough to cut may vary depending on what kind of soap you've made. Salt soaps can be unmolded after just a few hours, but most soaps need approximately 24 hours before they are hard enough to cut. Some recipes with a lot of liquid oils might need even more time, sometimes several days. Use protective gloves when you unmold and cut the soap, as it will still be rough against the skin.

Read more about cutting soap on page 120.

11. Zap test

If you want, you can do a zap test on the soap after 2 to 3 days by moistening a finger, dragging it against the soap, and quickly touching the finger to the tip of your tongue. The soap is not safe for use if you experience a small shock or "zap." If you do get a shock, wait a few weeks for the lye to react with carbon dioxide in the air and transform, then test again.

If it tastes only of soap (and that is not very tasty), the mixture is saponified.

12. Curing

The time has come to let the soap rest. Be patient. To give the soap the best shelf life, leave it in an airy space without direct sunlight for at least 4 to 6 weeks, preferably longer.

Recipes

There's an enormous demand for recipes but there are many bad recipes out there, even on the larger and otherwise dependable soapmakers' home pages. This is why you should enter each recipe into the soap calculator (see page 64) to make sure that the recipe works for you and determine if you need to make changes.

Here you'll find some of my favorite recipes and suggestions for additives. As soon as you change the type or amount of oil, enter it in the soap calculator and make adjustments if needed. It can be easy to forget how you made that fantastic soap a year ago when you're several soaps into soapmaking, so I recommend downloading the information for your own records. You won't have to recalculate the recipe if you only change additives; like an addition of a bit of clay or making the soap without essential oils.

I have chosen to include a large variety of recipes. With these, you can test out different soaps and change the recipe afterward depending on your personal preferences. I usually have about three go-to recipes I use, and only vary the additives. Eventually, you'll find your own favorite soaps.

All recipes are calculated using 1 pound (500 grams) oil, which is sufficient for a mid-sized loaf pan and will make approximately 6 to 7 soaps weighing around 2¾ ounces to 3½ ounces (80 to 100 grams). You can, of course, choose different scents or additives than what I recommend, but the soap batter's weight changes somewhat depending on which oils are included.

Coconut soap

This is a super soap to start with, and it is cheap to make, too. You'll get a really white and hard soap. As you only use one oil, the numbers in the soap calculator will look crazy. Just ignore them, because the soap will turn out great. To prevent the coconut soap from being too drying, it gets as much as 20 percent superfat. Soap from coconut oil traces quickly and saponizing starts early. Coconut soap batter turns very warm, so avoid using the oven for processing. It will probably gel by its own heat.

Recipe uses 1 pound (500 grams) oil; makes approximately 1½ pounds (725 grams) soap, with 20 percent superfat

4.79 ounces (136 grams) water
2.59 ounces (73.3 grams) NaOH (35 percent lye concentration)
1 pound (500 grams) coconut oil (100 percent)

0.55 ounce (15.5 grams) essential oil:
peppermint (30 percent)
lavender (40 percent)
palmarosa (30 percent)

Follow the step-by-step instructions on page 66.
Don't overblend. It is often enough to mix properly with the spatula. Pour the batter into a loaf pan or individual molds. Decorate with dried plants or if you want, make a pattern on top.
Don't wait too long to cut up coconut soap. It hardens quickly and is often ready to cut after just a few hours. Coconut soap is great for individual molds, as you can pop them out of the molds after a few hours.
Preferably cure the soap a bit longer (approximately 10 weeks) if you want a milder soap.

Bastille soap

This recipe contains a very large amount of olive oil, but it also has coconut oil to provide better lather and a shorter curing time.

Sodium lactate is a good additive for soap made with lots of olive oil because it produces a harder soap, but another alternative is salt water. Read more about how to use salt water in the recipe for salt water soap on page 100.

Recipe uses 1 pound (500 grams) oil; makes approximately 1½ pounds (695 grams) soap with 4 percent superfat

3.8 ounces (107.8 grams) water

2.54 ounces (72 grams) NaOH (40 percent lye concentration)

12.35 ounces (350 grams) (70 percent) olive oil

5.29 ounces (150 grams) (30 percent) coconut oil

0.55 ounce (15.5 grams) essential oil:
lavender (100 percent)
2 teaspoons green clay
1½ teaspoons sodium lactate (1.6 percent)

Follow the step-by-step instructions on page 66. Add the sodium lactate when the lye mixture has cooled to below 114.8 °F (46°C).

A super tip is to let this Bastille soap gel. Force gelling by placing the soap in the oven because it will harden quicker. Let the soap cure a long time, preferably several months. (I know, you need the patience of a saint when making soap!)

Bastille soap 2

This is a slightly more advanced recipe for Bastille soap. I recommend letting this one cure for a long time—at least 6 weeks—to get improved lather and shelf life.

Recipe uses 1 pound (500 grams) oil; makes approximately 1½ pounds (686 grams) soap with 4 percent superfat

3.62 ounces (102.6 grams) water

2.41 ounces (68.4 grams) NaOH (40 percent lye concentration)

12.35 ounces (350 grams) olive oil (70 percent)

2.65 ounces (75 grams) coconut oil (15 percent)

1.76 ounces (50 grams) cocoa butter (10 percent)

0.88 ounce (25 grams) castor oil (5 percent)

0.55 ounce (15.5 grams) essential oil:
lavender (100 percent)
2 teaspoons green clay
1½ teaspoons sodium lactate (1.6 percent)

Follow the step-by-step instructions on page 66. Add the sodium lactate when the lye mixture has cooled to below 114.8°F (46°C).

Aleppo soap

This cold process Aleppo soap uses olive oil and laurel berry oil to produce an antiseptic, mild, and remedying soap that also works well as a shampoo for dry scalps. If you don't like the heavy, somewhat spicy, and tar-like aroma of laurel berry, lower the amount of laurel berry oil and add a scent. This soap should preferably be cured for several months, up to a year. Adding sodium lactate or salt water will speed up the hardening process. Note that the soap's color changes from a green hue to a more yellowish color the longer it's cured.

Recipe uses 1 pound (500 grams) oil; makes approximately 1.46 pounds (664 grams) soap with 4 percent superfat

Follow the step-by-step instructions on page 66.

3.46 ounces (98 grams) water

2.35 ounces (65.5 grams) NaOH (40 percent lye concentrate)

14.11 ounces (400 grams) olive oil (80 percent)

3.53 ounces (100 grams) laurel berry oil (20 percent)

1½ teaspoons sodium lactate (1.6 percent)

Dish soap

Dish or cleaning soap is really a variation on coconut soap. It's up to you if you want to add baking soda, but it's good for dissolving fat. You don't want any excess fat on your dishes! That's also why it is so important to be very careful when you measure out the ingredients. It is good to have -1 superfat if you want to use essential oils. I'll show two recipes: one with essential oils and one without.

DISH SOAP, BASIC RECIPE
Recipe uses 1 pound (500 grams) oil; makes approximately 1.68 pounds (761 grams) soap with 0 percent superfat

6 ounces (170 grams) water
3.23 ounces (91.6 grams) NaOH (35 percent lye concentration)
1.10 pounds (500 grams) coconut oil (100 percent)
1 tablespoon baking soda

SCENTED DISH SOAP
Recipe uses 1 pound (500 grams) oil; makes approximately 1.72 pounds (780 grams) with -1 percent superfat

6.07 ounces (172 grams) water
3.26 ounces (92.5 grams) NaOH (35 percent lye concentration)
1.10 pounds (500 grams) coconut oil (100 percent)
1 tablespoon baking soda

0.55 ounce (15.5 grams) essential oil:
Litsea cubeba (60 percent)
peppermint (40 percent)

Follow the step-by-step instructions on page 66.

It is best to pour the soap batter into individual molds, as the batter hardens quickly. You can also pour the soap batter into containers (cups or jars), which you leave on the sink. Then, you can just moisten your washing-up brush when it is time to do the dishes.

To use the soap as an all-purpose cleaner, shred it with a grater and mix about ½ cup soap with approximately 4 cups (1 liter) warm water. Use it the same way as a soft soap cleaner.

To use the soap as a laundry detergent, grate ¼ cup (½ deciliter) soap and add this and ¼ cup (½ deciliter) baking soda to a laundry ball and put it in the washing machine.

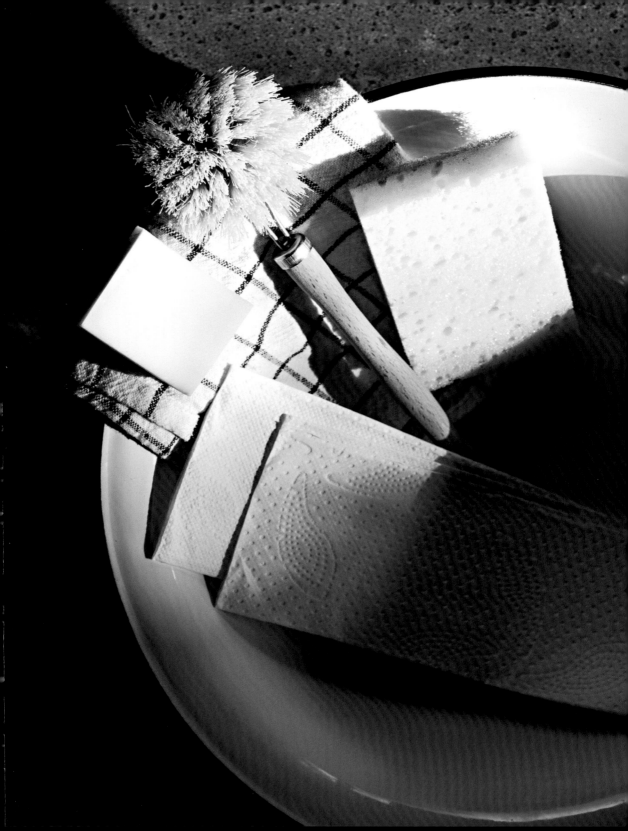

Citrus soap

This citrus-scented soap is made with three easy-to-find oils and is a cleansing soap because of the large amount of coconut oil.

If you want to use citrus slices to decorate the soaps, cut the fruit into thin slices and put them on a baking sheet. Place the sheet in a 212°F (100°C) oven and bake for 2 to 3 hours until they're dried out completely.

Recipe uses 1 pound (500 grams) oil; makes approximately 1.72 pounds (780 grams) soap with 5 percent superfat

4.66 ounces (132 grams) water
2.50 ounces (71 grams) NaOH (35 percent lye concentration)
9.70 ounces (275 grams) olive oil (55 percent)
5.29 ounces (150 grams) coconut oil (30 percent)
2.65 ounces (75 grams) canola oil (15 percent)

0.55 ounce (15.5 grams) essential oil:
orange (40 percent)
lemon (20 percent)
Litsea cubeba (20 percent)
clove (20 percent)
1½ teaspoons kaolin clay to anchor the scents
1½ teaspoons sodium lactate (1.6 percent)
Citrus of choice, sliced and dried

Follow the step-by-step instructions on page 66. Finely grate dried citrus peels if you want to add some scrub to the soap; it will also add some color. If you use a loaf pan, push some dried citrus slices into the soap batter for decoration.

For individual molds, place dried citrus slices on top of the soap. You can also place them in the bottom of the molds and carefully pour the soap batter into the molds.

Mild Earl Grey soap

I replace the water in this recipe with a strong Earl Grey tea, which I let cool completely before making the batter. I infuse marigold in all the olive oil in this recipe, which I let rest for a few weeks.

Marigold is a traditional medicinal herb often used in salves due to its anti-inflammatory and healing properties. It's not really known how much of the marigold's properties survive the saponification process, but it is a nice addition to this mild soap. If you want some scrubbing texture, add dried tea leaves to the soap batter.

Recipe uses 1 pound (500 grams) oil; makes approximately 1.53 pounds (695 grams) soap with 6 percent superfat

4.17 ounces (117 grams) water

2.22 ounces (63 grams) NaOH (35 percent lye concentration)

0.66 pound (300 grams) marigold-infused olive oil (60 percent)

3 ounces (85 grams) cocoa butter (17 percent)

3 ounces (85 grams) shea butter (17 percent)

1.06 ounce (30 grams) castor oil (6 percent)

0.55 ounce (15.5 grams) essential oil:
bergamot (70 percent)
palmarosa (30 percent)
1½ teaspoons sodium lactate (1.6 percent)
1 tablespoon dried and ground tea leaves

Follow the step-by-step instructions on page 66.

Divide the soap batter in half and mix the tea leaves into one half.

Soap with poppy seeds

Adding poppyseeds to your soap batter doesn't just result in great looking soap; it also adds an exfoliating effect. However, it is very easy to add too much, and make a far too abrasive soap, so less is more here. I like the contrast of black poppy seeds in a white soap, but you can color the soap after your personal taste.

Recipe uses 1 pound (500 grams) oil; makes approximately 1.51 pounds (687 grams) soap with 4 percent superfat

3.63 ounces (103 grams) water
2.42 ounces (68.6 grams) NaOH
  (40 percent lye concentration)
6.53 ounces (185 grams) olive oil
  (37 percent)
3.70 ounces (105 grams) coconut oil
  (21 percent)
3.53 ounces (100 grams) shea butter
  (20 percent)
2.65 ounces (75 grams) canola oil
  (15 percent)
1.23 ounces (35 grams) castor oil
  (7 percent)

0.55 ounce (15.5 grams) essential oil:
palmarosa (50 percent)
Litsea cubeba (50 percent)
1½ teaspoons sodium lactate
  (1.6 percent)
1½ teaspoons kaolin clay
Scant 1 tablespoon poppy seeds

Follow the step-by-step instructions on page 66.
Add the poppy seeds after you have mixed the soap batter.

Coffee soap

This wonderful soap is made with twice-brewed coffee and dried used coffee grounds as a scrub. First, I brew coffee as usual. Then, instead of water, I brew another pot using the liquid coffee from the first brew to get a really strong concentrate. The soap will be dark brown and have an amazing coffee aroma. If you want a lighter brown soap, brew weaker coffee. Freeze the coffee in ice cube trays before using it.

Dry the spent coffee grounds and add a little to the soap. Don't add too many coffee grounds, as it could make the soap too abrasive.

Recipe uses 1 pound (500 grams) oil; makes approximately 1.48 pounds (673 grams) soap with 4 percent superfat

3.67 ounces (104 grams) coffee, frozen in ice cube trays
2.45 ounces (69.4 grams) NaOH (40 percent lye concentration)
5.82 ounces (165 grams) olive oil (33 percent)

USE COFFEE BEAN OIL TO MAKE A MORE COFFEE-ACCENTUATED SOAP. THIS OIL IS EXPENSIVE BUT IT GIVES THE SOAP A STRONGER COFFEE SCENT.

3.88 ounces (110 grams) coconut oil (22 percent)
2.65 ounces (60 grams) canola oil (15 percent)
2.12 ounces (60 grams) cocoa butter (12 percent)
2.12 ounces (60 grams) shea butter (12 percent)

1.05 ounces (30 grams) castor oil (6 percent)
0.53 ounces (15 grams) coffee bean oil (3 percent)

1½ teaspoons sodium hydroxide
½ tablespoon dried used coffee grounds

Follow the step-by step instructions on page 66.
Add the frozen coffee ice cubes to a bowl, gradually pour the sodium hydroxide onto the coffee cubes, and stir. The coffee cubes will melt shortly. It can smell quite bad when the sodium hydroxide mixes with the coffee, but the smell disappears when the batter is saponified. Add the used dried coffee grounds either before or after trace.

Forest soap

I love the forest and its smell, so this soap is my personal favorite. It can be made with pine needle tea by boiling up a handful of pine needles and letting it cool. Another option is to make an extract from spruce or pine using either the shoots or needles. I made a spruce shoot extract by infusing shoots in the olive oil.

Recipe uses 1 pound (500 grams) oil; makes approximately 1.49 pounds (674 grams) soap with 4 percent superfat

3.68 ounces (104.5 grams) water
2.46 ounces (69.6 grams) NaOH (40 percent lye concentration)
6.17 ounces (175 grams) olive oil (35 percent)
4.41 ounces (125 grams) coconut oil (25 percent)
3.17 ounces (90 grams) shea butter (18 percent)
2.65 ounces (75 grams) avocado oil (15 percent)
1.23 ounces (35 grams) castor oil (7 percent)

0.55 ounce (15.5 grams) essential oil:
pine needle (40 percent)
juniper (30 percent)
cypress (20 percent)
Amyris (10 percent)
½ teaspoon green chromium oxide or spirulina or 1½ teaspoons green clay
1½ teaspoons kaolin clay

Follow the step-by-step instructions on page 66.

Separate the soap batter into two halves. Color one half with the chromium oxide, spirulina, or green clay and the other with kaolin clay. Pour the green soap batter into the pitcher with the white soap batter (or pour white into green, as the order doesn't matter here). Mix the soap batter a few times with a spatula to mix the colors a bit.

Pour the soap batter back and forth along the sides of the mold.

Facial soap with activated charcoal

Activated charcoal is a well-known product used to treat skin impurities, but face soap is a tricky subject because a soap that is great for one person might be too dehydrating or too greasy for someone else.

This recipe produces a mild soap for normal to dry skin that's also great as hand soap, but it contains a lot of unsaturated fatty acids, so add salt or sodium lactate to increase hardness.

Recipe uses 1 pound (500 grams) oil; makes approximately 1.55 pounds (703 grams) soap with 5 percent superfat

4.30 ounces (122 grams) water
65.9 g NaOH (35 percent lye concentration)
9.70 ounces (275 grams) olive oil (55 percent)
3.53 ounces (100 grams) almond oil (20 percent)
2.65 ounces (75 grams) cocoa butter (15 percent)
0.88 ounces (25 grams) castor oil (5 percent)
0.88 ounces (25 grams) coconut oil (5 percent)

0.55 ounce (15.5 grams) essential oil:
tea tree oil (100 percent)
2 teaspoons activated charcoal

Follow the step-by-step instructions on page 66.
Separate the batter into two parts. Mix activated charcoal into 1.20 pounds/543 grams (80 percent) of the soap batter and leave the rest of the batter white.
Pour the black soap batter into the mold first, then pour the white part in lines, back and forth along the length of the mold, from varying heights.

Salt soap

Salt soap removes dead skin cells, helps against acne, eczema, and psoriasis, and removes odors that are hard to remove with plain soap. Salt soap is also a good facial soap. Unfortunately, salt kills bubbles. We compensate for this with a high level of coconut oil. As a result, the consistency of the lather is creamy rather than bubbly.

To be a true salt soap, the amount of salt must be between 50 and 100 percent of the oils' weight. Use fine-grain salt, i.e., table salt (non-iodized), sea salt, or Himalayan salt. Avoid Epsom and Dead Sea salts.

It is best to use individual molds because the large amount of salt in this recipe makes the batter set very quickly.

Recipe uses 13.05 ounces (370 grams) oil; makes approximately 1.57 pounds (713 grams) soap with 20 percent superfat

3.37 ounces (95.5 grams) water
1.81 ounces (51.4 grams) NaOH (35 percent lye concentration)
10.44 ounces (296 grams) coconut oil (80 percent)
2.61 ounces (74 grams) olive oil (20 percent)
6.53 ounces (185 grams) salt (50 percent)

0.40 ounce (11.4 grams) essential oil:
lavender (40 percent)
sage (40 percent)
myrrh (20 percent)
1½ teaspoons pink clay

Follow the step-by-step instructions on page 66.

Add the salt to the soap batter when it starts to trace.

Pour the batter into individual molds. Make sure to check the batter after a few hours if you use a loaf pan and cut the soap before it gets too hard.

This recipe is calculated to give just about the same weight-ready soap as other recipes in this book, but the oil weight needs to be adjusted due to the large amount of salt. Calculate your soap mold like this:

First, enter the recipe in a soap calculator according to the usual amount you use for your mold, without salt and with 20 percent superfat and 35 percent lye concentration. This is to get the maximum weight allowed for the soap batter. Using the same mold I've used for this book's recipes, it takes approximately 1 pound (500 grams) of oil to get 1.65 pounds (750 grams) soap batter. With 20 percent superfat, the total soap weight would be slightly lower at 1.57 pounds (714 grams) because a smaller amount of oil would be saponified and therefore demand less water and sodium hydroxide.

If you want to make a salt soap with the salt weight at 50 percent of the oil weight, you'd add the total salt weight to the total soap weight: 1.57 pounds (714 grams) + 8.82 ounces (250 grams) = 2.13 pounds (964 grams).

If that's too much batter for your soap mold, you'd need to calculate what percentage of each ingredient needs to be decreased to make the soap batter fit your mold by dividing the desired amount by the excessive amount: 1.57/2.13 (714/964) = 0.74 (74 percent). This means you'd use 74 percent of recipe ingredients to arrive at the right amount, salt included.

Multiply the oils' weight (even the essential oils) by 0.74 to arrive at the new oil weight, which is 13.05 ounces (370 grams) in this example. The salt percentage is then 50 percent of the new oil weight: 6.53 ounces (185 grams).

Enter the new oil weight in your soap calculator. Pull up the recipe and check that the sum is correct. In this case, the total weight for the soap batter before curing ought to be 1.16 pounds (528 grams) + salt (6.53 ounces/185 grams) = 1.57 pounds (713 grams).

This calculation works for any mold you want to use. You just need to know how much soap batter your mold will hold.

Saltwater soap

Saltwater soap is different from salt soap, in that salt soap contains much more salt and the salt is added at trace, giving the salt granules an exfoliating effect, while saltwater soap is made with just saltwater, which can be incorporated in all kinds of recipes. Because this recipe calls for the salt to be dissolved in water, it will create a hard, white soap with creamy lather.

It's fine to use a salt percentage up to 25 percent of the water weight. You can also make this soap using seawater, which contains about 3.5 percent salt, but remember to use the cleanest seawater possible. Avoid water along popular beaches or built-up areas. The salt makes the lye slightly milky white, which is perfectly normal.

Recipe uses 1 pound (500 grams) oil; makes approximately 1.52 pounds (689 grams) soap with 5 percent superfat

3.67 ounces (104 grams) water

0.37 ounce (10.4 grams) salt (10 percent of water weight)

2.45 ounces (69.4 grams) NaOH (40 percent lye concentration)

8.82 ounces (250 grams) olive oil (50 percent)

4.59 ounces (130 grams) coconut oil (26 percent)

3 ounces (85 grams) shea butter (17 percent)

1.23 ounces (35 grams) castor oil (7 percent)

0.55 ounce (15.5 grams) essential oil:
peppermint (35 percent)
sage (35 percent)
frankincense (30 percent)

$2/5$ teaspoon ultramarine or indigo

Mix the salt and measured water until the salt is completely dissolved.
Follow the step-by-step instructions on page 66.
Then, divide the soap batter into two parts and mix one part with
4.87 ounces/138 grams (20 percent) blue color pigment.
Pour the white soap batter into the mold. Then, pour the blue batter from a
7.85-inch (20-centimeter) height back and forth along the mold's length.

Rosy clay soap

This is a delightfully scented soap made with clay and sunflower oil. Many soapmakers like to use sunflower oil, but it's an unstable oil, so the risk for dreaded orange spots (see page 127) increases. In this recipe, the linoleic and linolenic acids come to exactly 15, which is the maximum allowed for these fatty acids to avoid the soap turning rancid. Make sure that your sunflower oil is as fresh as possible. I have also decreased the superfat to lower the risk for rancid oil.

Rose oil is difficult to extract, making it very expensive. It is made as an absolute, which is stronger and more potent than essential oils. If you like, you can use an artificially scented oil and it will make your costs much lower. The clay gives a nice color and has a soothing effect. I use lilac clay with a pinch of red clay.

Recipe uses 1 pound (500 grams) oil; makes approximately 1.53 pounds (692 grams) soap with 3 percent superfat

3.74 ounces (106 grams) water
2.49 ounces (70.6 grams) NaOH (40 percent lye concentration)
7.58 ounces (215 grams) olive oil (43 percent)

4.42 ounces (125 grams) coconut oil (25 percent)
2.65 ounces (75 grams) shea butter (15 percent)
1.76 ounces (50 grams) sunflower oil (10 percent)
1.23 ounces (35 grams) castor oil (7 percent)

0.55 ounce (15.5 grams) essential oil:
rose absolute/French rose (70 percent)

lavender (30 percent)
2 teaspoons lilac, pink, or red clay (I use lilac mixed with about ⅕ teaspoon red clay)
⅕ teaspoon activated charcoal
1½ teaspoons sodium lactate (1.6 percent)

Follow the step-by-step instructions on page 66.
Separate the soap batter into two parts and mix the activated charcoal into the smaller part. I use 4.83 ounces/137 grams (20 percent).
Pour the darker batter into the mold, then carefully pour the lighter batter on top.

Soap on a rope

It's practical to use a string to hang up your soap. Something else that's handy is to attach a champagne cork to the string to make the soap float if you drop it in water. I like to attach strings to smaller soap cubes.

I use coffee grounds and a hint of vanilla in this recipe. It isn't possible to extract pure vanilla essential oil, but it exists as an absolute and as vanilla oleoresin. These are expensive, but very concentrated, so I use only 2 percent of the recipe oils' weight. This recipe has high levels of coconut oil and shea butter to produce a hard and cleansing soap.

Recipe uses 6.91 ounces (196 grams) oil; makes approximately 9.56 ounces (271 grams) soap with 5 percent superfat

1.45 ounces (41 grams) water
0.97 ounce (27.5 grams) NaOH (40 percent lye concentration)

2.77 ounces (78.4 grams) olive oil (40 percent)
2.08 ounces (59 grams) coconut oil (30 percent)
1.59 ounces (45 grams) shea butter (23 percent)
0.48 ounce (13.7 grams) castor oil (7 percent)

0.21 ounce (6 grams) essential oil:
vanilla oleoresin (100 percent)
½ tablespoon dried used coffee grounds
½ teaspoon sodium lactate (1.6 percent)
Hemp or jute string

Follow the step-by-step instructions on page 66.
Add the coffee grounds after mixing the soap batter. Pour batter into the mold. Wait until the batter isn't too runny, then insert four pieces of string into four different places in the soap. Make loops by poking down both ends of the strings, or alternatively, insert only one end if you want to tie the other end to a cork.

Beer produces a very nice lather, and the response is usually very positive when you explain that, yes, the soap really is made from beer. Any beer will do the trick. A dark stout will give a dark brown color, while a lager will make a lighter soap.

Beer soap

Using beer in soapmaking is a bit more advanced because it demands a few extra steps in the preparation, and a bit more caution, but beer is a true favorite in soapmaking, even with the extra work. (A tip: I use up the leftover beer friends leave behind after our parties.)

This soap batter can trace quickly, so don't plan on adding sophisticated patterns the first time around.

Any recipe will work. Just go ahead and replace the water with the same amount of beer. It is important to remember that the sugar in the alcohol will make the lye concentration very warm.

You'll need to dealcoholize the beer, which is done by simmering it over low heat. Simmer the beer for about an hour. The smell might not be the greatest, but it is quickly done and this way the beer also becomes stale. Let it cool, then freeze it in cube trays.

Recipe uses 1 pound (500 grams) oil; makes approximately 1.57 pounds (713 grams) soap with 5 percent superfat

4.49 ounces (130 grams) beer
2.47 ounces (70 grams) NaOH (35 percent lye concentration)
6.35 ounces (180 grams) olive oil (36 percent)
4.59 ounces (130 grams) coconut oil (26 percent)
3.17 ounces (90 grams) shea butter (18 percent)
2.29 ounces (65 grams) canola oil (13 percent)
1.23 ounces (35 grams) castor oil (7 percent)

0.55 ounce (15.5 grams) essential oil:
orange (50 percent)
vetiver (30 percent)
patchouli (20 percent)
1 teaspoon cocoa

Prepare the beer a day in advance by simmering it on the stove for an hour, then freezing it in ice cube trays.

Follow the step-by-step instructions on page 66.

The smell is nauseating when beer and sodium hydroxide are mixed, but the smell disappears during saponification. Add the sodium hydroxide to the frozen beer cubes gradually so that the cubes melt when you stir.

Separate the soap batter into two parts and mix the cocoa into one part. Pour the colored batter back into the pitcher holding the uncolored batter. Stir a few times with a stick or spatula, then pour the batter into a mold.

This soap usually needs one or two extra days before you can cut it.

Honey & oats

It's incredibly popular to make soap with oats and honey. This recipe is more advanced, so you ought to have tried soapmaking at least a few times before jumping in here because honey contains loads of sugar that makes the soap batter enormously hot, risking a volcano eruption or burning of the batter if you don't work fast enough.

It is possible to use all oat milk instead of water, but the consistency turns jelly-like when the milk is mixed with sodium hydroxide. That's why I have chosen a slightly higher amount of water, where half of the water is mixed with sodium hydroxide, and the other half is replaced with oat milk, which is added gradually.

It is a good idea to saponify at a lower temperature, maximum 98.6°F (37°C), to make sure that the batter doesn't overheat. When I made the soap pictured here, the lye concentration was at 104°F (40°C) and the oils were at 93.2°F (34°C).

Recipe uses 1 pound (500 grams) oil; makes approximately 1.57 pounds (710 grams) soap with 4 percent superfat

2.47 ounces (70 grams) water

2.47 ounces (70 grams) oat milk

2.43 ounces (69 grams) NaOH (33 percent lye concentration)

8.11 ounces (230 grams) olive oil (46 percent)

3.53 ounces (100 grams) coconut oil (20 percent)

2.65 ounces (75 grams) shea butter (15 percent)

2.29 ounces (65 grams) almond oil (13 percent)

1.06 ounces (30 grams) castor oil (6 percent)

1½ teaspoons sodium lactate

1 teaspoon finely ground oats or colloidal oats

1 teaspoon honey

Prepare the oat milk one day in advance or a few hours before soapmaking by mixing oats and water in a ratio of 1:10, i.e., 1 tablespoon oats to 10 tablespoons water.

Stir or blend the mix and let it rest for a few hours or overnight. Strain through a cheesecloth or sieve to avoid large pieces getting in the mix. It doesn't really matter if some oats end up in the soap because it will make the soap more exfoliating.

Continue by following the step-by-step instructions on page 66.

Once the lye and oils reach around 98.6°F (37°C), pour the lye into the oils and stir. Add the colloidal or finely ground oats before mixing.

In a separate bowl, mix the honey with a small amount of warm water until it dissolves. Once the batter has reached light trace, add the honey water and blend for a second or two to mix properly.

This is the moment the soap batter can start to darken and turn red from the warmed honey, so work fast.

Pour the batter into the mold and decorate with oats. To make a honeycomb pattern design, carefully press Bubble Wrap down on the surface of the batter. Quickly place the soap in the freezer and leave it for a few hours. Check on it now and then. You can move it to the refrigerator or another cool area and leave it overnight.

Move the mold to room temperature the next day. The soap might need to rest an extra day to harden sufficiently.

Tar soap

Tar soap is a treatment soap to use now and then rather than as an everyday soap. This soap's smoky scent makes it perfect for the sauna! Use 100 percent wood tar, never coal tar. The tar should be made from pine trees. You can use 2 to 15 percent tar in this recipe. The more tar you add, the quicker the batter will trace. Pine oil works well but is heavily concentrated, so don't use more than 5 percent. This soap is not for a beginner soapmaker because the tar makes the soap trace incredibly fast.

The tar scent can be rather pervasive, so store the soap in a secluded place if you are sensitive to smells. No additional scent is needed, as the tar scent is so strong, but if you still want to add something, spruce and juniper needles are a good match.

Tar colors the soap a lovely brown.

There are two important things to remember when you make tar soap to make the process go smoothly: Don't let the soap batter get too hot (around 89.6°F/32°C works well to slow down trace), and don't use an immersion blender for tar soap; use a whisk or spatula instead.

Recipe uses 1 pound (500 grams) oil; makes approximately 1.54 pounds (698 grams) soap with 4 percent superfat

4.20 ounces (119 grams) water
2.26 ounces (64 grams) NaOH (35 percent lye concentration)
9.70 ounces (275 grams) olive oil (55 percent)
2.65 ounces (75 grams) cocoa butter (15 percent)

2.65 ounces (75 grams) coconut oil (15 percent)
1.76 ounces (50 grams) pine tar (10 percent)
0.88 ounce (25 grams) castor oil (5 percent)

0.55 ounce (15.5 grams) essential oil:
spruce needles (50 percent)
juniper (50 percent)

Follow the step-by-step instructions on page 66.

Measure the tar and mix it with the oils before
mixing with the lye.

Pour in the lye once both oils and lye are at around
89.6°F (32°C). Stir thoroughly with a spatula to
mix the lye properly with the oils. You'll pretty
soon feel the batter start to trace and become
thicker. Add essential oil(s) if using, mix some
more, then pour the batter into a mold.

Shampoo bar

This recipe uses beer due to its vitamins and proteins, but you can also use water or apple cider vinegar. Apple cider vinegar is acidic and neutralizes some of the lye, resulting in a shampoo bar with a higher superfat level. If using apple cider vinegar, enter 2 percent superfat in your soap calculator. You can replace the total amount of water with apple cider vinegar or divide the water amount as in the Honey & Oats recipe on page 109.

Recipe uses 1 pound (500 grams) oil; makes approximately 1.54 pounds (700 grams) soap with 3 percent superfat

3.9 ounces (110 grams) beer
2.59 ounces (73.4 grams) NaOH (40 percent lye concentration)

9.17 ounces (260 grams) olive oil (52 percent)
6 ounces (170 grams) coconut oil (34 percent)
1.23 ounces (35 grams) castor oil (7 percent)
1.23 ounces (35 grams) cocoa butter (7 percent)
1½ teaspoons sodium lactate (1.6 percent)

0.55 ounce (15.5 grams) essential oil (lavender, rosemary, sage, peppermint, and chamomile are some good essential oils traditionally used to strengthen hair)

Prepare the beer in advance by simmering it on the stove for an hour, then freezing it in ice cubes.

Follow the step-by-step instructions on page 66.

Lotion, bath bomb & exfoliant scrub

Now that you have the different ingredients for soapmaking, let's take the opportunity to make some other cool items: a lotion bar to lubricate hands and body; a softening bath bomb to use in the bathtub; and a super quick peeling exfoliant.

LOTION BAR

These simple lotion bars warm in your hands. As they soften, they can be used to moisturize your body.

1.16 ounces (33 grams) coconut oil (33 percent)

1.16 ounces (33 grams) shea butter (33 percent)

1.16 ounces (33 grams) beeswax (33 percent)

0.04 ounce (1 gram) essential oil of choice (1 percent)

Melt the coconut oil, shea butter, and beeswax in a water bath. Stir until everything is melted and mixed. Add the essential oil. Let the mixture cool a little and pour it into individual molds; ice cube trays work well for this purpose.

For a vegan recipe, replace beeswax with rice wax, candelilla wax, or carnauba wax. If you choose to use carnauba wax, use half as much as the beeswax amount, i.e., 0.58 ounce (16.5 grams).

SKIN-SOFTENING BATH BOMB

Epsom salt contains lots of magnesium, which creates a relaxing effect. Use finely ground salt to avoid too big granules.

0.88 ounce (27 grams) baking soda (27 percent)

0.88 ounce (27 grams) citric acid (27 percent)

0.88 ounce (27 grams) Epsom salt (27 percent)

0.63 ounce (18 grams) coconut oil (18 percent)

Approximately 0.04 ounce (1 gram) essential oil (1 percent)

Mix all ingredients until the consistency resembles damp sand. You can make small balls or press the mix into molds. Let the bath bombs rest a few hours in the refrigerator or a day or so at room temperature. Place a bomb in the bathtub and take a bath!

EXFOLIATING PEEL/SCRUB

This super-fast peel can be thrown together in just a few seconds. Use it to exfoliate your body and lips to remove dry skin.

1 tablespoon sugar or Epsom salt (33 percent)

1 tablespoon coffee grounds (33 percent)

1 tablespoon coconut oil or almond oil (33 percent)

Mix all ingredients. Done! The peel/scrub crumbles a bit, so use the scrub over your sink or in the shower. This peel/scrub will last several months stored in an airtight container.

Cleanup & Tips

Before I wash my used pitchers and utensils, I scrape them out thoroughly with a spatula to collect any leftover batter to make more soap.

Depending on how quickly the recipe hardens, adapt the scrape timing so that the batter doesn't get too hard. It varies from recipe to recipe. I use up the leftovers by making small balls, which I then cure with the rest of the soap I just made. They become perfect small soap balls, or can be reused in some kind of ball confetti soap (see page 132).

The remnants on the utensils will turn into soap within a day or two, becoming so much easier to clean. Clean the dishes in warm water first, then once again with some dish soap to get rid of the last of the oil. Avoid using the dishwasher. (You don't want to mix soapmaking equipment with food utensils!) Your dishwasher won't be happy with soap and oil residues.

CUT THE SOAP

After one to two days (sometimes longer depending on the recipe), unmold the soap and cut it up. You can use a kitchen knife, a tightened guitar string, or a tool specially designed for soap cutting. A dough scraper works as well. If you notice the soap's interior is a bit too soft, wait an extra day.

If you have topping on the soap, cut the loaf on the side, otherwise the knife will drag the decoration and mark the soap as you cut.

GRATE & SHAVE

You can shave the soap as soon as you've cut it up, but I usually wait until it has hardened some more.

I use a common vegetable peeler and press ever-so-lightly along the sharp edges. I save the trimmings and reuse them either in confetti soap or in a soap bag. Use everything; nothing needs to go to waste.

Grate soap with a grater if you want to make some cleaning or liquid soap. Mix it with water before using.

STORE THE SOAP

Soap needs to cure for at least four weeks. Store it where the air circulates freely and not in direct sunlight. A wire storage basket is suitable, or on a shelf. Avoid placing the soap directly on uncoated metal, as it can produce oxide rings. Try to space the soap with gaps in between each bar so that each bar gets air on all sides.

Cover the soap with a light fabric like muslin to avoid dust accumulation on top.

SOAP BAGS

You can buy ready-made soap bags in various materials, sew your own bags from linen or an an old curtain, or crochet one from strong string. I've even made soap bags from a loofah!

SHELF LIFE

If soap can't dry out in between uses, it will go bad. That's why a good soap dish is important. It's really the be-all and end-all for a soap's shelf life.

A soap dish needs holes for drainage. However, as soon as a soap dish retains some water, it becomes a bad dish. Some wooden soap dishes absorb humidity, which means that the soap still rests against a damp surface during a prolonged period. Soap ought to have as little surface contact on the bottom as possible to allow air to circulate.

A good way to allow air circulation is to let the soap rest on some kind of brush, like a nail brush or a vegetable brush. A piece of loofah is good, as is an irregular stone to allow the water to drain off.

Preferably, alternate between two to three different soaps, allowing them to dry properly between uses. If yours is a multi-person household, it is especially important to have many soaps, perhaps a soap for each person.

Storage, humidity, recipe, soap dish, and usage all affect a soap's shelf life. A soap that's cured a few weeks will usually last about one month with normal usage by one person.

Create simple patterns

There are many fantastic pattern techniques in soapmaking. Some are easier while others are very intricate and difficult. Even if they turn out totally different from what we wanted, soap patterns often yield fabulous results.

For soaps that I cut and don't like, I put aside someplace where they are not constantly in front of me. When I return to them after a few weeks, I'm nearly always positively surprised to see that the soaps aren't so bad looking after all.

That said, pattern techniques are difficult to master, and it is even more difficult to get two soaps to look identical, so here are a few easier techniques to start with.

DROP SWIRL

This easy pattern will give varied but fine results each time. The pattern can be made with just two colors or as many colors as you want. The challenge here is making sure the soap batter doesn't gel far too much before you have time to pour.

Keep a light trace and divide the batter into the number of colors you want. Mix in the color pigments thoroughly. You can add a main color to a larger part of the soap batter or add all the colors in equal amounts.

Pour all the colors back into the pitcher, pouring along the pitcher's side from different directions if you like. Stir once or more with a stick or spatula. Try out different techniques to see the effects. The colors mix more as you stir, and the transition is less noticeable once the soap is ready. Pour the batter into the mold. I usually pour back and forth along the length of the mold.

TWO-TONE

Using two-toned colors is a classic pattern technique in soapmaking. You can, of course, use more colors, but that also means a bit more work.

Start with medium trace in the soap batter. Divide the batter in two and color both parts as desired. Pour the first layer into the mold and smooth it out evenly. If you want a straight horizontal separation between the two colors, tap the mold against the work surface to make the batter settle flat.

Pour the second layer on top, pouring carefully to prevent the second layer from penetrating the first. It works well to pour the second layer against a spatula held at an angle above the first layer, as it slows the batter's speed. Pour the same way along the mold.

HANGER SWIRL

A classic way to create this pattern is to use two colors, 80 percent of a main color and 20 percent of a contrasting color.

First, pour a layer of the main color. Then, carefully pour the contrasting color across the middle in a horizontal line. Now, pour another layer of main color. Continue in this fashion until you've run out of the contrasting color.

You can also simplify by pouring the main and contrasting colors at random. You'll get a pattern regardless.

Take a metal hanger and push it into the soap batter, either in the middle or along the side. You can push the hanger to the middle of the batter, then sidewise, then pull it up again, or push it to the bottom, drag it to the side and up and down again, then drag it to the other side and up again.

What you're doing is mixing the soap batter in the mold to vary the pattern in many ways. Mix lots or do just a half sweep. Once you've finished, tap the mold against the work surface. If needed, fix the top to look good.

PENCIL LINE

A patterned line going straight through a bar of soap looks good, whether it's completely straight or irregular.

First, choose a color pigment. Certain pigments might bleed a little from the line, but mica pigment works well, as does a small amount of activated charcoal. Spirulina is good, too.

You will need a light to medium trace in the soap batter. Divide the batter into two parts and color them if you like.

Pour the first part of the batter into the mold and smooth the batter, or leave it irregular for a more lively line. Use a tea strainer and sprinkle the selected color pigment along the whole soap.

It's not necessary to cover the whole surface because it might be difficult to cover the sides of the mold. It's also more attractive if the batter isn't completely covered.

If the batter hasn't thickened enough, hold off until it has. Carefully pour the second part of the batter, guiding it along a spatula, down over the color pigment. It's a bit tricky to get this perfect the first time around because color pigments have a tendency to move around, but it should still look good!

Troubleshooting & corrections

SODA ASH

Soda ash is a white powdery layer on a soap's surface. It appears when sodium hydroxide in the soap reacts with carbon dioxide in the air, creating sodium carbonate. It is extremely common, not dangerous, and only affects the look of the soap. It should disappear after a few uses.

To prevent the formation of soda ash, reduce the recipe's water content. Less water makes the soap harden faster, reducing the risk for creating soda ash. In my experience, it is usually reduced when there is a 40 percent lye concentration.

Also, make sure your soap is not exposed to too much air in the beginning. After pouring it into the mold, cover the soap batter as soon as possible. Make sure the batter is kept evenly warm by placing it in the oven or wrapping a blanket around the mold.

If this doesn't do the trick, once it is in the mold, try adding a thin layer of rubbing alcohol (as pure as possible) over the batter. The alcohol creates a protective layer so that soda ash doesn't form. Add rubbing alcohol after pouring the batter into the mold and again after half an hour.

Another solution is to decrease the superfat to between 2 and 4 percent if you've used a higher superfat than this.

If soda ash has still developed on your soap, wait until it is hard, then wash the soap with water or rubbing alcohol. Use a soft brush or, if you have a steamer, try to carefully steam off the soda ash. Keep the steamer about 4 inches (10 centimeters) from the soap for about 30 seconds. The soap will turn nice and shiny.

You can also simply rinse the soap in cold water once it has cured. Use gloves to avoid leaving finger imprints.

PARTIAL GELLING

A partial gelling might happen if you don't force gelling by putting the soap batter in the oven or wrapping the mold to keep it evenly warm. The soap batter then gels where it is warmest, i.e., in the middle. Since a soap's color is affected by gelling, when you cut up the soap, there may be a dark round ring in the area of the partial gelling. This ring is purely aesthetic (if even that), and the soap is still usable.

That said, even if you have just cut the soap, you can try forcing gelling by putting the soap back in the mold, turning the oven to maximum 158°F (70°C), and leaving the soap in the oven for an hour. After an hour, turn off the oven, leave the oven light on, and let the soap cool down slowly.

DOS, DREADED ORANGE SPOTS

DOS are small orange specks or spots that appear on your soap if the soap oils have oxidized or turned rancid. You run a greater risk for DOS if your soap recipe contains a high level of unstable oils. A general rule is that, together, linoleic and linolenic acid should not have a higher value than 15 in your soap calculator. Any oils used should also be fresh, not past their "best by" dates. Hard water contains minerals and metals that can cause the oil to go rancid. There is also an increased danger for DOS if a high level of superfat is used.

The risk for DOS increases if the soap is stored in a humid environment or where the humidity from the soap can't evaporate properly. DOS can appear during curing or later.

It is perfectly okay to use soap with DOS, but the soap might start to emit a bad smell and become slimy, and that is not very appealing. Some soapmakers use citric acid in soap to counteract the appearance of DOS.

TOO SOFT

Soaps containing a lot of liquid oils need a long time to harden, especially if you didn't use salt or sodium lactate in the recipe. You might have also used too much water. To get the right amount of water in the recipe, I use a lye concentration between 35 to 40 percent.

Another reason for too-soft soap is that you may have used too little lye. The superfat is then higher and that produces a softer soap. The soap will still be useable—just cure it an extra-long time.

CRACKS

The most common reasons for cracks in soap are the soap contains too much hard butter and wax, the soap got too warm, or both.

Another possible reason for cracking is the soap might be "lye-heavy." When a soap is lye-heavy, too much lye was added during the soapmaking process, resulting in a dry soap.

Lye-heavy soap is safe to use for house cleaning or doing dishes, but not for your skin.

CRUMBLY

Soap can be crumbly because you waited too long to cut it, you added too much salt or sodium lactate, or the soap is lye-heavy, i.e., there is too much lye that never underwent saponification. This might be the reason if you didn't use any salt at all.

Use lye-heavy soap to clean surfaces or wash dishes but do not use it on your skin.

NO LATHER

Some soap recipes, like olive oil soap, just don't produce a lot of lather, but here are some suggestions to increase lather in most soaps. Lauric acid, found in coconut oil, promotes good lather. If possible, increase the coconut oil in the recipe.

Castor oil makes the lather stable (use 6 to 7 percent and all the way up to 10 percent), or use 1½ teaspoons PPO sodium lactate to help with the lather.

Sugar is another remedy (1 teaspoon sugar, honey, or milk). You could also try using less superfat—try 4 percent.

VOLCANO

A volcano can occur if the oven is too warm when you place the soap inside or if you've used ingredients that contribute to heating the soap batter, like different sugars.

Don't heat soap batter in the oven if you use sugars in the soap. Don't heat coconut oil soap in the oven either. If you use a lot of sugar, you'll probably need to place the soap in the refrigerator or freezer instead, for anywhere from four to twenty-four hours.

GLYCERIN FLOODS

A lot of water or liquids in a soap recipe can produce glycerin floods. This shows up as translucent light lines or patterns. Glycerin floods are purely an aesthetic issue but if you want to avoid them, decrease the amount of water in your recipe.

AIR BUBBLES

It is very easy to inadvertently incorporate air into soap batter. To avoid this, try mixing batter with your spatula more and less with an immersion blender. If using an immersion blender, lean it to the side and downward when you insert it into the soap batter to help remove air under the blender head. Then, lean the blender toward the middle so that the blender stands upright in the batter as you mix.

After you've poured the batter into the mold, tap the whole mold against your work surface or drop the mold from a height of 12 to 15 inches (30 to 40 centimeters) onto the floor to help dislodge air bubbles from the soap batter.

WHITE SPOTS

When cutting soap, you may discover small white spots that are caused by stearic acid and palmitic acid, i.e., hard and solid fatty acids. To avoid white spots, try a slightly warmer soap batter and make sure all hard oils and butters are completely melted before they are added in.

THE BATTER DOESN'T TURN INTO SOAP

Various things can prevent batter from turning into soap. It's possible for the oil to separate in the mold, or there could be pockets with oil or lye inside when you cut the soap.

A false trace can also prevent batter from turning into soap, as well as not having mixed the oils and lye thoroughly (preventing the saponification process from starting or finishing).

You can recognize when soap is lye-heavy if lye is in the pockets. This soap is only fit to be thrown out.

Save the soap

Sometimes soap turns out really ugly. It may not look or smell like what you had envisioned or there could be some weird things happening to it. Perhaps it traced too quickly and turned lumpy or puke-like or the oils separated. I suggest letting some time pass and checking on the soap down the line. Chances are that you can still rework the soap using any of the following methods.

THE OUT OF SIGHT, OUT OF MIND METHOD

This is the simplest solution for aesthetic eyesores: hide the soap. A closely woven soap bag makes sure that you never need to see the soap again.

RE-BATCH—HOT PROCESS

This method can save a soap when, for example, you have forgotten an oil, a scent, want to change color, or something similar.

Hot process requires a slow cooker for the simplest and safest procedure. Grate in the soap and stir until it melts and starts to gel. Then, add what you feel was missing and pour the batter back into the mold. You might also need to add some water to the grated soap while you stir.

This soap will be coarser than a cold process soap. Use safety equipment and be careful because the soap batter will be very warm.

CONFETTI METHOD

This is a very simple way to repurpose grated soap and bigger soap pieces. It is best if all soap pieces used are as similar as possible so that they don't separate with use.

Recipe calculation—the complicated but more exact method

To calculate the new amount of soap you're making, you first have to weigh the confetti you want to use.

Start by entering your usual recipe in a soap calculator. As an example, I'll take a mold that holds about 1.65 pounds (750 grams) soap batter before curing. The oils' weight is rounded to 1 pound (500 grams), which means that about 70 percent of the recipe is oils. This is the same thought process as when you have to calculate the volume of a new mold.

In our example, we're using 5.29 ounces (150 grams) confetti. We're calculating the confetti's oils by multiplying the confetti by the recipe's oil percentage: 5.29 × 0.70 = 3.70.

The confetti therefore contains 3.70 ounces (105 grams) oils.

Now, we take our original oil weight, which is 1 pound (500 grams) for this recipe, and subtract the confetti's oil weight: 500 − 105 = 395 grams (13.93 ounces).

Go to the soap calculator and enter the new weight, 13.93 ounces (395 grams) under "Total weight of oils."

CONCLUSION
- The confetti's weight multiplied by the soap's oil percentage equal the weight of oils in the confetti
- The soap recipe's oil weight minus the confetti's oil weight equals your new recipe's oil weight

Recipe calculation—the "make it up as you go" method

If you don't want to bother with calculations because you hate doing it as much as I do, just make it up as you go. Decrease the recipe a little bit, around

3.53 ounces to 7.05 ounces (100 to 200 grams) to make a smaller amount of new soap batter. Add the soap confetti. Either you're in luck, and it is just the right amount for your mold, or you get smaller soap. Possibly, you get too much soap batter. That's when it's good to have another small mold on hand to use up the excess soap batter.

THE CIAGLIA METHOD

With this method, you grate unsuccessful soap and mix to get as smooth a batter as possible. You'll make a new but smaller batch of soap from this. The grated soap can be freshly made, or you can use an older soap.

Use up to 40 percent grated soap for the new recipe. The new soap recipe ought to have a fatty acid combination as close as possible to the original recipe.

Add the grated soap to the oils and blend until smooth before adding the lye. To calculate how much grated soap is needed, take the percentage you want, for example 40 percent, and multiply this by the weight of the oils in the recipe you usually use for the particular mold you're going to use: 1 pound/500 grams ($0.4 \times 500 = 200$ grams) and that will make 10.58 ounces (300 grams) of new soap batter.

Index

THANK YOU

to Jenny, who initially explained soapmaking; to my mother, my brothers; to Amanda, Felicia, Natur & Kultur; and to all friends who cheered me on and tested soap for this book. And a thank you to myself, because I dare to continue my experiments.

Skyhorse Publishing books may be purchased in bulk at special discounts for sales promotion, corporate gifts, fund-raising, or educational purposes. Special editions can also be created to specifications. For details, contact the Special Sales Department, Skyhorse Publishing, 307 West 36th Street, 11th Floor, New York, NY 10018 or info@skyhorsepublishing.com.

Skyhorse® and Skyhorse Publishing® are registered trademarks of Skyhorse Publishing, Inc.®, a Delaware corporation.

Visit our website at www.skyhorsepublishing.com.

10 9 8 7 6 5 4 3 2 1

Library of Congress Cataloging-in-Publication Data is available on file.

Print ISBN: 978-1-5107-7769-9
Ebook ISBN: 978-1-5107-7770-5

Printed in China